The Flip of a Coin

114 Years in Alaska

The Flip of a Coin

114 Years in Alaska

Doris Tobin Bordine

ꞐORTꞍBOOKS

Eagle River, Alaska

Photo Credits: Personal collection of author

Cover design: Julie Christensen, Creative Visual Marketing
                Solutions, Anchorage, Alaska

Cover background photo:
                Tobin Pass, vicinity of Wiseman, Alaska, named
                after August Tobin

Other: *The Alaska Journal*, Bob Henning, Publisher (p. 66)
                The Tenacious Emery Tobin, Louise Brink
                Harrington (p.152)

Published by:

ᘉORCᕼBOOKS

11915 Lazy Street, Ste. C
Eagle River, Alaska 99577
www.northbooks.com

Printed in the United States of America
ISBN 978-0-9830764-7-6
Library of Congress Control Number: 2012944916

Dedication

1897–1989

I lovingly dedicate *The Flip of a Coin* to the memory of my Aunt Florence Tobin Thornton, who made the publication of our family memoirs possible by her translations and chronicling of Grandpa August's life and experiences.

Aunt Florence was as big an influence in my life as my parents. She fed me, like in her picture to the left, not only with physical food but with a desire to learn. Her interest in our family when my husband was going to college and seminary was generous and always positive. Her travel adventures sowed the seed for my hunger for travel and exploring the world.

It was Aunt Florence who taught me how to use a typewriter and allowed me to hack away on her own machine even though I constantly piled up the keys. Since she had no children, she considered me her surrogate child and spent much of her time playing games with me, taking me fishing off the dock, and teaching me with flash cards she made.

Thank you, Aunt Florence, for your loving influence on my life.

Contents

Part One

Chapter 1   3
  Living in Sweden and America

Chapter 2   21
  '98 Gold Rush Changes Everything

Chapter 3   41
  August's Life Above the Arctic Circle

Part Two

Chapter 4   95
  After Twenty Years, Son Meets August in Ketchikan

Chapter 5   112
  Roots Are Planted in Ketchikan

Chapter 6   123
  World War II Upsets It All

Part Three

Chapter 7   143
  Third Generation Makes Alaska Home

Chapter 8   160
  Midwest Parish Life

Chapter 9   176
  Back to Alaska

Chapter 10   185
Return to First Love: Printing

Chapter 11   193
Shishmaref Calling

Chapter 12   205
Change in Travel Plans

Epilogue   214

Acknowledgments

Since many of the stories in this book took place over a hundred years ago, many, many folks have had a hand in preserving them. Even though I do not know who they all are, I am deeply grateful to all of them.

My gratitude goes first to my aunt, Florence Tobin Thornton, who in the 1930s interviewed my grandpa, August Tobin, and wrote down his adventures in the far north.

I deeply appreciate my father, Emery Tobin, for writing and presenting a speech commemorating the seventy-fifth anniversary of the Gold Rush of '98. I especially appreciated his comments on how this exciting era affected our family's future.

Ketchikan author, Louise Harrington, expertly used material about our family to write about my dad, his character and work toward the betterment of Ketchikan. I am indebted to her for permission to use her writing.

I am also most thankful for my writing group's encouragement, suggestions, and the inspiration of their own writings shared at our weekly meetings. They are Louise Freeman-Toole, Stephanie Jaeger, Arlene Lidbergh-Jasper, Debbie Cutler, Lizzie Newell, Marilyn Blumer, Morgan Grey, Cindy Bell, and Dianne O'Connell.

The technical, inspirational, and encouraging support of Ray and Jan Holmsen of Northbooks has been the catalyst that got this book into print.

I also felt much encouragement from my many friends who always asked how my book was progressing.

Thanks to you all. It's been a long time a-comin' but it would never have been finished had I not had your help.

Introduction

Grandpa August Tobin was physically present in the first eight years of my life, but he has always been a giant personality to me my whole life. His children, my dad, Emery, and my aunt, Florence, always spoke of him as a hero who endured severe hardships in the north with unwavering stamina. His wife, Emma, my grandmother, also portrayed him as a hard-working, loving husband and grandpa any child would love.

Since our family was in the magazine publishing business, one would think that many of Grandpa's stories would have been printed in *The Alaska Sportsman* but, evidently, it was a situation like the proverbial shoemaker's children without shoes, and Dad put off writing the stories, thinking he'd do it after retirement. When he retired, Dad was more interested in writing about political and social matters in letters to the editor.

It was Aunt Florence who managed to write down the stories as Grandpa told them in the 1930s. She was interested in being a good writer and took many classes to polish her skill. The stories retold in this book are vivid examples of her talent. Robert Marshall commented in his book *Arctic Village* about folks in Wiseman, "John (sic) Tobin, oh, what a liar he was!" Perhaps August was known to be a storyteller who embellished the truth, but our family understood his stories as gospel.

I tried for many years to find a writer who would take Aunt Florence's writings and put them in book form. Finally, I accepted the fact that I wouldn't find anyone, and it must be up to me to do the job. It was in the writing group that I joined that I was urged to continue our family story by including my folks' and my memoirs. I thought no one would be interested in my story until I realized that maybe looking back on my eighty-two years might reveal some surprising history to readers.

Alaska has always meant a land of opportunity whether it was gold to be found or a business to be started. In my early years I believed if one had a good business idea, his chances of making it a success were much better in Alaska because chances are no one else had thought of doing it yet. As for adventure, it was easy to go out into the country and imagine that you were the first to have ever been there. We felt secure during the depression, because like the Southeast Alaska collection of oral histories titled *Clams on the Beach, Deer in the Woods* implies, we knew there would always be enough food for us even if we had no money to buy it.

There was prosperity for anyone to grasp if he just persevered, I thought. Like Grandpa's experience, that fortune may not be the one for which he is searching. In his case, living in Alaska with family turned out to be his wealth.

Celebrating God's grace,
Doris Tobin Bordine
July 2012

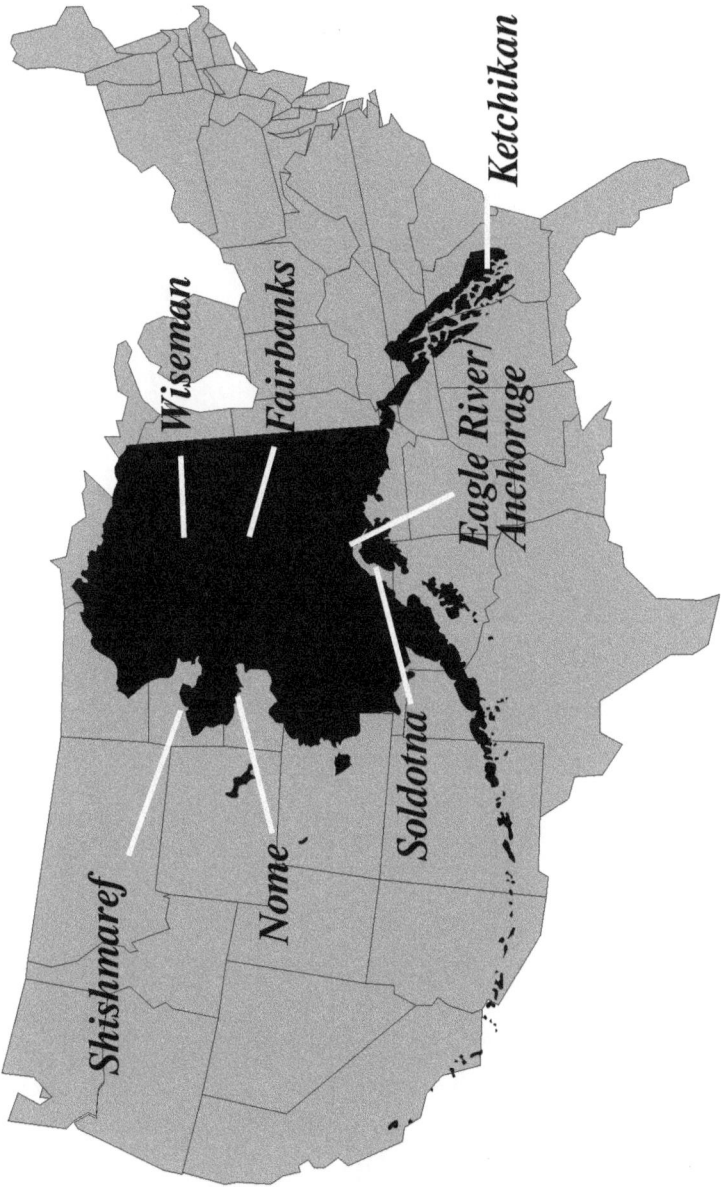

Shishmaref

Nome

Wiseman

Fairbanks

Soldotna

Eagle River/
Anchorage

Ketchikan

How Big Is Alaska?

Part One

Chapter 1

Living in Sweden and America

This letter from Winnie Creek, Alaska, to Boston, Massachusetts, took a total of about two months: From Winnie Creek to Circle: eighteen days; from Circle to Skagway: thirty days; and from Skagway to Boston, MA: twelve days. It no doubt went much of the way by dog team.

Words in parenthesis are mine, to make the meaning clearer. In some cases, Dad skipped words, and in other cases, he did not finish his sentences. His spelling is that of Sweden eighty years ago. Swedish spelling has been greatly simplified. The bold face words are his, and so are the exclamation marks.

Florence Tobin Thornton
April 9, 1968

Winnie Creek
North Fork of Koyukuk River, Alaska
January 23, 1900

My loving little wife,

I had a few words from Carl today written July 27, 1899. He said he sent a letter to St.

Michael—too bad. He does not say whether you are alive or dead. I have not heard from Miller, nor a word from you since I last wrote. Soon, I'll have been in Alaska two years!

Think! I hope though that you and our little ones are alive and well. Under the circumstances it is hard for me, but the hardship for you at home is much worse than for me.

However, it is difficult for me, too. When my thoughts go out to you, a shudder goes through my body when I realize I don't know how you are. If I only knew, **knew,** that you were all right! As for me, I feel fine—haven't had a sick day; have felt very well indeed, here.

My fortune is in the ground. How much my claims are worth I cannot say, but no one could buy me out for $100,000. No! I dream of millions. Six of the 18 claims my partner and I have are fully paid for.

Not all claims are rich by any means. Therefore, I am convinced that the one (claim) is enough, (because a quarter mile is a long way to go) and therefore it is difficult to get out any gold, or to open up some of the other claims (especially) now because foodstuffs are practically nonexistent around here.

Flour is $57.00 a sack, pork $140.00 a pound and those are the prices minus cost of delivery.

We have (enough) food, until June, thanks be—also wood. And then no doubt the steamer will come, and will go all the way up (the river).

No one is working now. It will be summer diggings that we will open up No. 1 above Discovery (Creek) and No. 13 at Winnie (Creek).

I do not know whether you will get this or if you received the previous money (I sent). The last time (I sent money) was two months ago when I went down for supplies. As soon as the river (breaks) open I'll send you some more, so that you can take care of yourself until I get ahead in the fall. Although I don't have dollars now, and must be in debt to those who have, I am sure we have gold (judging) from the little we have taken out with pick and shovel, But that is nothing (compared to what we will take out). I can do laborer's work now and then. Wages will be higher in summer, surely from $15 to $20 a day.

Tell Carl that for certain that what he put out will be repaid. Soon we will have ample money, but I wish that you would not tell anyone of my circumstances, except to our very closest friends. Well, you understand, of course, that it does not concern anyone else, anyway.

If an accident should happen to me, and it could happen, it would be very bad (painful?). Men have died here among my so-called friends.

How is the little boy?—big now, I guess, and the little girl. Oh! If only I could see them for a half an hour—how wonderful that would be—or if I could be home! I think almost every moment of the day of that time!

I will write to Carl next time there is an opportunity. I think that this (letter) will go out overland to Dyea. I have only a short time to write, but at least you will receive these few lines, but I will start a long letter in a few days and will send it when opportunity comes and now I send my affectionate greetings to Carl, Knut and family, and also to your other sisters and theirs. Warm kisses to you and our little ones.

From your own,

/signature/

August

P. S. We now have three U.S. (land) commissioners here and soldiers are on the way, so I think we will soon get mail regularly.

Write soon and often. Ask Carl to write (also). A.

* * * * *

Who is this man writing from seventy-five miles north of the Alaska Arctic Circle to his family in Boston, Massachusetts?

His story begins in Sweden.

"In 1865 the last of September was the first of August," August used to joke when asked when he was born. He loved to josh with folks, and relished walking up to a stranger and in a very consoling voice say, "I hate to be the one to tell you this. It makes me very sad. I hope you can take the bad news: I'm a better looking man than you are!"

His jovial nature was possibly a way he had of coping with the severe atmosphere he grew up in. August was born on the southwestern Swedish island of Käringön. Like its surrounding islands and mainland, it had been scraped and polished by ancient glaciers until now it looked like a giant whale, sunning its back that has broken through surface of the water. One could fear that the next high tide, pushed by a North Sea storm, might wash away all the little red homes clinging to the smooth rock. Käringön, probably derived from *cairn*, a Scottish word meaning "heap of white stone markers," took the name, perhaps, because of the navigational markers on the far side of the island. Some, however, say Käringön means "old woman," and the island was named that because they were the only persons left when all other able-bodied residents went out fishing.

Adding to the bleakness of the surroundings was Pastor Simson, a tyrant of a pastor who ruled the settlement with an iron hand, armored with Old Testament legalism. With strong conviction, Simson decreed that too many of the residents' names ended with "son," so he decreed that "Tobiason," for instance, be shortened to "Tobin." His own name was exempt.

He had been assigned to Käringön because of its reputation as a very rough and less than sober community, like many of the settlements in the area. He was commissioned to make the inhabitants more God-fearing and law-abiding. Simson thought that changing their names would help the residents adopt a new and more docile lifestyle along with a new name.

When August was eight years old, his mother died giving birth to her sixth child. Ignoring the fear and sorrow that engulfed the community, and especially August and his family, Pastor Simson preached the message he thought appropriate.

Imagine how August felt when he heard his beloved mother described as such a weakling, and her gender being responsible for the fall of man in the Garden of Eden. Yet, there was hope: she had borne children, a redeeming act, AND the family would see her again in heaven. BUT SOON?

Sermon Oration in 1873

Pastor Laurentz Olaf August Simson (Lutheran pastor at Käringön from 1850 to 1910) published a small paper-back volume of what he considered his best sermons and tributes after 50 years of ministering to the inhabitants of Käringön.

One of the talks was given at the funeral services of Grandmother Emilea Tobin (or Tobiason) who died at age thirty-seven when our Dad was only eight years old.

I copied it from the pamphlet in possession of Fridolf. Probably the only copy on the island.

Florence Tobin Thornton,
1-10-69

Sermon

There must be something that defends a woman's salvation. That she is the last to be created by God, is the weakest, and has the least strength to do that which would oppose evil is true. Women do not have the firmness, steadiness, strength and power or the natural reliance on the body that men have. Since women are weaker than men in body so it is the same in relation to her soul, and its salvation.

Women are by nature thankless, ungrateful, fickle, and easily caught, easily fettered, easily persuaded, and easily moved towards good and bad. They do not have the inward strength to fight against anything bad as men have. God's word tells of women's love as though it were the weakest there is. Therefore, the devil worked through the woman to direct them (Adam & Eve) out of paradise. It was

9

the woman's fault—not the man's. And after he had won her to his side, he won over the man.

Since humans have such a strong and firm enemy as the devil, in the world and the flesh, it is the women who are weak and bend to the evils as did their original Mother Eve, and the devil well knows how to tempt the flesh, so he uses Woman who is ready and willing in his world. Therefore, it seems extremely difficult if not impossible for a woman to obtain salvation.

That which seems to champion woman's salvation is childbirth. From I Samuel, 4:20: "And about the time of her death the women that stood by her said unto her, 'Fear not; for thou hast borne a son.' But she answered not, neither did she regard it."

And from I Timothy 2:14-15: "and Adam was not deceived and became a transgressor. Yet women will be saved through bearing children if she continues in faith and love and holiness with modesty."

Therefore, through a woman's childbirth the world's Savior came to the world because of sin of mankind as well as to pay for woman's sins, and nothing can further hinder her salvation.

It will also be a strong spur [hope?] for us since we know we will sometime soon meet

the loved one and the one we will so miss and
we will embrace her as Women can become
saved by childbirth, because both before and
during and after it, God's breath, and power
is at work. So one can have cause to hope (or
have deep hope) for a woman, that in childbirth, she will be saved.

So the deceased, after having broken her bap-
tismal vow returns to the Lord through her
love, holiness, with chastity, demonstrated to
His throne. This we know because of God's
word. She died in childbirth through which
she has gained salvation. This should be for us
a sign for happiness and thanksgiving, we who
bear the sorrow and the loss. It will also be a
stronger spur [hope?] for us since we know we
will sometime soon meet the loved one and
the one we will so miss and we will embrace
her as David did his Jonathan.

(Note: The son born to Grandmother Tobin,
Ernst Yustus Teofilus, lived but 12 days.)

Because he always was acting for the good of the
community, in his own way of thinking, it is easy to believe in the myth that Simson demanded that every boat
going to the mainland bring back a sack of soil so that
they could plant vegetable gardens and also eventually
have a graveyard beside the church.

Parents went to him to find out what punishment
would be appropriate for their children's misdeeds. The

children were drilled with Bible memorization so that they would know right from wrong.

Hunger was not a stranger to August because his father sometimes dipped into the grocery money in order to finance celebrating with other fishermen when they came in from long successful fishing days or to drown their sadness after poor fishing days.

When August and his friend found eider duck nests with eggs, they immediately gathered as many as they could and cooked some over a little campfire at the far end of the island.

They carefully carried the surplus home, thinking they would appease hunger pangs again someday. August must not let his stepmother know about them because she would certainly disapprove.

When he thought of the perfect hiding place, he felt very proud of himself. He hid the eggs in the pockets of his father's frock coat. He knew it would not be taken out of the closet to wear until there was a special church holiday service to attend. Easter had passed so they'd be safe for a long time, he thought.

But only a few weeks later, he saw his stepmother whacking the coat outside on the clothesline. She was beating the dust out of it to have it ready for Pentecost services. August had forgotten about Pentecost! Of course, it wasn't long before the hidden eggs had turned into a slimy mess.

August was hurried off to Pastor Simson for appropriate discipline.

"Where in the Bible does it say you can steal eggs from wild birds?" thundered Simson.

August feared the worst. He'd stood before the towering taskmaster many times before to recite chapter after chapter of the Bible from memory during Bible classes.

Shivering from fright, he stuttered, "Deuteronomy, chapter 22, verses six and seven. It says there," he continued, "if any bird's nest chance to be before thee in a way, in any tree, or on the ground, whether they be young ones or eggs, and the mother sitting upon the eggs, thou shalt not take the mother with the young, but thou shalt in any wise let the mother go, and take the young (or eggs) with thee that thou mayest prolong thy days."

No one had ever witnessed Pastor Simson obviously at a loss for words before. Finally he spoke, "That was in the Law of Moses. Not ours. You know your Bible well. You are pardoned. Go, and do no wrong again."

It was not long, however, before August was in trouble again. Church services were usually four hours long. Children were not excused from these marathon rantings of Pastor Simson's. August was gifted with an artist's skill. He often came prepared with pencil and paper and slyly sketched the parishioners as the sermon droned on.

One particular Sunday he found himself in luck when the island's most homely man, asleep, was slumped as if to pose for the young artist. His face, adorned with a huge hooked nose, warts protruding, was a perfect subject for August's pencil and paper. When finished, the portrait, more of a cartoon, was passed along the pews.

When he finally got home, the sketch was handed to him by his stepmother. One look at her face and August knew he was in for some rough punishment.

"Disgraceful!" she shouted. "Drawing pictures of good people and making fun of them . . . and in church, at that!" She whipped him many strong strikes with the handy branch kept for that purpose. He was, once again, sentenced for the rest of the day to the attic to sit among several coffins stored there. He knew his punishment was to appease the wife of the man he'd drawn.

Several weeks went by, and the man in the drawing became ill and suddenly passed away.

Grief-stricken, the widow meekly sought out August, as he was mending his father's fishing gear. Sweetly, she said, "Be a good boy and let me have the sketch you made of my husband. I have no picture of him."

"My stepmother destroyed the picture," August said, looking the other way to hide the glee on his face.

"But you'll draw me another won't you?" the widow pleaded.

"Never!" August replied. "I suffered too much for drawing the first one."

* * * * *

House painting was a good trade to learn on this little weather-beaten island where homes needed painting frequently. August began learning the trade as a teenager but didn't stay at home after he was seventeen. He took off for the bigger cities to become a journeyman after the two-year apprenticeship. When in Stockholm, he got a contract to paint all the buildings on the nearby estate of a wealthy family, the Lowens. It was there at Djursnesgard, Oaxen, that he met Emma.

Emma Erickson was the oldest of six children born to Louisa Catherine (Patterson) Erickson and Carl

Anders Erickson. She was born in Nykoping, but the family moved to Oaxen, where father Carl worked in a lime plant for a time but found he could do better at carpentry. Many lime workers needed houses, and he could not only build them but also draw the plans for them. He was a good provider but, of course, they put no money aside in savings, so it was a great financial blow when he died just after their twins were born.

Louisa could not manage to care for all six of her children, so she was forced to find a home for two of them: Emma, age eleven, and Ottelia, age seven. She knew they would have a better life than she could provide, yet it was a heart-wrenching decision to have to make.

"It was as if my heart were torn from my chest to give you and Ottelia up the same year I lost my loving husband," she told Emma.

Madame Karin took Emma who soon began lovingly calling her *Tant* Karin, using a term for persons who were not related but like part of the family.

Baroness and Baron Lowen, who owned the Djursnas Estate, wanted Ottelia to live with them like their own child. When Ottelia saw the buggy with the baroness' nursemaid coming to fetch her, she ran and hid, but she soon was found because her sobs were easily heard. The nursemaid picked her up, avoiding being kicked by Ottelia's protesting little feet. She put her in the cart among boxes of clothing that had been purchased for her by her new family.

Soon mother Louisa left the estate with the other four children to return to Nykoping where she owned a little house. Her sister came to help with the twins who were less than two years old. Nykoping was not far from the Djursnas estate, so Emma, along with Ottelia, was able to visit now and then. Even sister Elin, when she was only eight or nine, learned to signal for a boat to pick her up and take her to the island of Osmo to visit her sisters. Brother Carl, too, visiting friends at Djursnas, dropped in on his sisters still living there where a lime plant was the main employer. They kept pretty close contact with each other.

Tant Karin was a very busy lady. She ran the estate dairy farm and supervised two hired girls, thus she could pay the tuition for a better school for Emma. This meant Emma had to row alone across the bay for classes. Sometimes it was too stormy to return home for several days, so she stayed with the teacher who was also a seamstress and happy to teach Emma her skill.

When Emma was thirteen, she stopped going to school because she was told, "That's all we can teach you."

The two-year, twice-a-week confirmation classes continued. Walking six miles twice a week, sometimes through waist-high snow, kept her in good shape. After confirmation, Tant Karin took Emma on a trip to many well-known places in the area of Stockholm, just as she would if Emma were her own birth child.

Emma was glad when she could get jobs sewing for neighbors, the baroness, and her hired hands. Emma would stay at these homes for several days, often sewing into the early morning hours in order to finish a garment for a special occasion. Contributing money for the household expenses made her feel good.

At age nineteen, Emma had many suitors but none she was particularly interested in. She'd been told by many that she was quite good-looking. Then one day a very handsome chap came to the estate from the Gothenburg area. Everyone was talking about him because it was unusual for someone to come from so far.

One particular day Emma, dressed in her best to go to a christening with Tant Karin, was riding a beautiful horse and towing a decorated cart: a lovely sight for a young nineteen-year-old man. He followed her until she stopped to visit with an acquaintance of his. He saw to it that they were introduced. Although she'd been curious about his name for days, she didn't catch it when the introduction was first made. She shyly asked his name again and repeated, "August Fridolf Laurentius Tobin! What a name!" It soon didn't matter if she remembered his whole name, because he made sure they met frequently when only first names mattered and even those were put aside for more endearing ones.

Friends knew that Emma had been seeing Bernard Bloomquist, and he was considered her sweetheart. She had fun teasing each of her suitors by praising the attributes of the other one. August went along with the teasing by describing imaginary girlfriends he had back home.

After only three months of this jolly courting, August told her his work on the estate was finished, and he was going home to Käringön. It was then that Emma realized she loved him. Three months later he wrote to her that he was going to America with a friend who had come back home from there for a visit.

A short time later, Carl, now nineteen, wrote for Emma, twenty, to come home to Nykoping because their mother was very sick. The steamers were laid up for winter, so Emma had to wait for them to begin their routes again. When Carl met her on the pier, she could tell by the look on his face that she was too late. Her mother had died an hour before the ship docked. It was 1886.

At that time, there were no undertakers to help with the funeral arrangements, so it was up to the two siblings to bathe and dress the body, buy a coffin, arrange for the funeral services, and prepare food for the mourners. But that was not the worst. The two of them had to make arrangements for the care of their four younger siblings.

The twins were now nine years old. *Moster* (aunt) Johanna volunteered to take Axel but not his twin sister Alma. Unfortunately, Johanna tired of caring for him after a few weeks, so he went to another family who was paid by the city for his care. That situation was very tough and as soon as he was fifteen, he went to sea, and then to America to be with his brother Carl.

At Baroness Lowen's advice, Emma went to the governor's wife for help in finding an orphans' home for Alma. Alma stayed there until she went to America at age sixteen. Ottelia, also, by that time had crossed the Atlantic to find a new life.

Now only Elin and Emma remained in Sweden. Emma felt she could not leave ailing Tant Karin alone with no one to care for her, even though August was coaxing her in each of his letters to join him.

August was building a good painting business. Governments were over-spending money on all kinds of projects. When it was decided to re-gild the capitol dome of Boston, August won the contract. The Swedes were experiencing the good life they'd dreamed of.

Good news of their success came in every letter to the sisters. The brothers worked in restaurants and dreamed of having their own business some day. The sisters worked for wealthy families who were very generous, on occasion giving them extra furniture and food. So seven years after August left, it was not surprising that Elin decided to leave for America and a new life. Emma could not envision being the only one of the siblings left in Sweden.

August sent a ticket for each of the sisters. The twenty-two-dollar cost of each was about a day's wages. Tant Karin wanted Emma to remain and marry a local man and take care of her. With tickets in hand, though, the desire to follow her heart was too strong for Emma to remain beside Tant Karin.

She and Elin boarded the old MV *Venetia* in Gothenburg on May 2, 1894, and were off on the fifteen-day voyage to America. It was a stormy crossing in a ship so old that it was decommissioned shortly after arriving in New York. This rotting ship made their misery many times worse. The accommodations on board were crowded and the food so poor that the sisters were ravenous when they docked, and they gorged themselves on so many bananas they got sick. But after two days they were well enough to board the train to Boston.

What a welcoming party awaited them! There at the train station, all dressed in their best, were the girls' sisters and brothers and many friends who had immigrated too. Best of all, in Emma's eyes, was that handsome, jolly guy August. In the past seven years he had

19

grown from a playful young man into a gentleman of the world. It would take awhile for Emma to get used to this self-confident person. She was sure she'd made the right choice in crossing the Atlantic, yet she didn't want to marry right away. She had to be sure they were still in love.

Emma was happy to see that August and her brother Carl were good friends. Carl, too, had a sweetheart, Hilma, and the four decided to have a double-ring wedding. They chose the date: November 10, 1894. It was six months after Emma arrived. The effects of the Panic of 1893 had not yet filtered down to the middle class.

Suddenly, the effects of the bankruptcy of the Reading Railroad, which had been expanding beyond its means, and the extravagance of government that took gold reserves down to scary minimums began to be felt, and the results of the Panic of 1893 were dire. Unemployment reached 18.4 percent. August had to lay off his employees. His creditors were slow in paying, and August could not cover his debts. Yet, Emma felt fairly secure living near her siblings who always helped each other out. By pooling their resources, they were all able to live a fairly comfortable life at first, but when the panic descended on them with full force, it caused the newlyweds to fear for their future.

Adding to the expenses, but bringing much joy to the Tobins was the birth of Emery Fridolf on December 14, 1895. Following, eighteen months later on May 9, 1897, was Florence Emma. Carl and Hilma, also, had two children.

Chapter 2

'98 Gold Rush Changes Everything

The following is the partial script of a talk, revised by the author, given by her father, Emery Tobin, to a Vancouver, Washington, community gathering to commemorate the seventy-fifth anniversary of the 1898 Klondike Gold Rush.

The Gold Rush
By Emery F. Tobin
1973

The Klondike hangs behind me like a theatrical backdrop, haunting my dreams and memories.

The discovery of Klondike gold had a profound effect on this country. It changed Alaska and that legacy is part of our heritage.

This year marks the seventy-fifth anniversary of the start of the great stampede of men called the Klondike Gold Rush. It reached its peak in 1898.

Seventy-five years ago this country was in the depths of a depression into which it had been sinking for thirty years. It was now a panic! People hoarded gold to such an extent that the United States Treasury, which had previously held $730,000,000 in gold was down to $90,000,000. Debtors were unable to pay their creditors. There was a general sense of fear and hopelessness.

What the people did not know yet was that on August 17, 1896, an event occurred on a remote stream in Canada's Yukon Territory that would electrify the country and much of the world. The stream was called Rabbit Creek, later renamed Bonanza. It flowed into the Klondike River.

The news of the discovery was to bring hoarded gold out of hiding from socks and sugar bowls and set the wheels of industry turning as they had not turned for thirty years.

But the event was in such a far-off, uninhabited, sub-arctic region that it was not to become generally known for eleven months.

That was when two steamers made port— one in California and the other in the state of Washington. The *Excelsior* docked in San Francisco on July 15, 1897, and the *Portland* in Seattle two days later.

Tipped off by the arrival in Frisco of men laden with Yukon gold on the *Excelsior*, enterprising Seattle editors sent reporters out to meet the *Portland* at sea.

The result was that when the *Portland* docked, newspapers were already on the streets with screaming headlines proclaiming the arrival of a TON OF GOLD. They were not exaggerating! The grimy prospectors on the *Portland* were actually carrying ashore more than TWO TONS of gold in sacks, suitcases, and boxes—all from the fabulously rich Klondike region of Canada!

The man who had made the exciting discovery was George Carmack. History, however, has also given credit to Bob Henderson as co-discoverer because he pointed out the creek to Carmack, telling him where to look.

Carmack was a pioneer of an earlier gold rush—to California. He was a genuine sourdough, married to the daughter of a Tagish Indian Chief.

It was the policy of the old-timers for anyone discovering gold to reveal the location to his friends. Henderson was working on Gold Bottom Creek. He told Carmack that he thought there should be a rich paystreak on Rabbit Creek, just across the divide from where he was working. Rabbit Creek, like Gold Bottom, is a tributary of the Klondike River.

Henderson advised Carmack to try Rabbit Creek and let him know if he discovered anything. Carmack promised to do so. He went to Rabbit Creek with two Indian friends. It was there on Rabbit Creek that Carmack, in the company of Skookum Jim and Tagish Charlie, discovered gold between the flaky slabs of rock like cheese in a sandwich.

A ten-cent pan would have indicated a good prospect. There the gold went four dollars to the pan! They shouted and danced with joy around the discovery. Each man was soon to realize a fortune that made him wealthy for the rest of his life.

But, although Carmack heralded his discovery far and wide, he failed to notify Henderson as he had promised to do. This was because Henderson, in parting, had made an insulting remark about Carmack's two Indian friends.

Henderson was busy on his own little claim. He missed out on the subsequent wild rush to stake the rich ground. He eventually went home broke.

By August 1896, all the ground in Rabbit Creek, now called Bonanza, had been staked.

Other prospectors, arriving daily, fanned out across the Klondike watershed.

A young Austrian immigrant named Antone Stander made another electrifying discovery on a nearby creek. It became known as El-dorado. Charles Lamb staked a claim which he was to sell for $350,000. Charles Lippy, a former Seattle YMCA physical education instructor, staked claim sixteen. It produced $1,530,000 for Lippy.

Nobody knew it at once, of course, but Eldo-rado turned out to be the richest placer creek in the world. Almost every claim, from Num-ber 1 to Number 40 was worth at least half a million. Some were worth at least three times that amount. And a quarter century later, dredges would still be taking gold from the worked-over gravels.

Is it any wonder then, that when eleven months later the news finally reached the Outside (the lower forty-eight states), the country went wild. Gold seekers hurried to go to the Klondike. They expected to get rich quick.

Pacific Coast ports competed with each other to attract gold seekers. They wanted the travelers to outfit and go north through San Francisco, Portland, Tacoma, Port Townsend,

Seattle, Victoria and Vancouver, B. C. as well as other ports.

Seattle proved to be the most successful in luring the gold seekers. The Chamber of Commerce hired a veteran newsman of subtle ingenuity named Erastus Brainerd. Brainerd left nothing to chance in promoting Seattle as the port to sail from. He advertised and sent news stories far and wide. The transportation companies followed suit.

Whaling was poor, so whale boat owners advertised for passengers. The fare on a whaler, if you could get passage, was two hundred dollars. Some men paid as much as fifteen hundred dollars when tickets were hard to get.

In a single week in mid-August, twenty-eight hundred persons left Seattle for the Klondike. By September first nine thousand persons and thirty-six thousand tons of freight had left the port. Every city on the coast was a madhouse. In all, more than one hundred thousand men took part in the rush for gold.

Thousands were frozen in during that first winter. For them, it often took eight to ten months to reach Dawson, in the Klondike. When most of the delayed argonauts reached that mad city of gold, they found that all creeks had been staked. In disgust, they threw

away the outfits they had so laboriously assembled to come North. They took the first
ships south.

Surprisingly, however, many would not give
up. Many went to nearby Alaska. Some
remained in the North the rest of their lives.
Now in 1973, a few in their nineties are still
there.

The story of the Gold Rush is remarkable in
many ways. One is that in an extraordinary
number of cases, the industrious and sober
prospector profited little from the gold fields,
while the ne'r-do-wells and the profligates
often amassed great, if temporary, wealth. For
many it was easy come, easy go.

Even the mayor of Seattle, W. D. Wood,
caught the gold fever. He resigned his post,
formed a company of prospectors, and went
North. Preachers, lawyers, bankers, doctors,
merchants, farmers, young men, old men,
strong men, weak men, gamblers, bunco art-
ists, robbers, pimps, and entertainers joined
the stampede. The girls went too. Those of
the dance-hall variety and those who could
not dance. They came from all the states as
well as Canada, Scandinavia, Australia, New
Zealand, and other far corners of the globe.
The lunacy that resulted is incredible.

The lives of millions were changed. The stampeders spent millions of dollars and thousands of toilsome hours in the search for the yellow metal. It has been estimated that more money was put into the search for gold than was taken out.

There cannot possibly be any exaggeration of the hardships, the dismay, sorrow, sickness, and death that resulted from the efforts of the men to reach the gold fields.

The easiest but the longest route to the Klondike was to sail three thousand miles across a part of the Pacific Ocean, the Gulf of Alaska, and the Bering Sea to the mouth of the Yukon River. Then, sail seventeen hundred miles up the Yukon to Dawson, but the Yukon was open to riverboats only a few months of the year, from June to September.

False reports were circulated by the transportation companies in efforts to get the prospectors to sign on their vessels. Whaling boat captains who were familiar with the route to the Arctic falsely reported gold on the beaches of Kotzebue above the Arctic Circle.

The gold seekers spread out in all directions in the Yukon and Alaska. They crossed mountain ranges, pulled small craft up roaring rivers, over rapids, and crossed huge glaciers.

Some even sledded supplies over the terrifying Malaspina, the largest piedmont-type glacier outside of Greenland. One party dragged an eight hundred-pound engine over this crevassed ice sheet, only to abandon it in the trees when they finally got across.

They suffered starvation, scurvy, fatigue, frozen limbs, and soaking wetness. They lived through the winters in little log hovels, crowded like sardines in a can, encased in sleeping bags for weeks at a time. But nothing deterred these determined, frenzied men from their resolve to get to the gold fields at any cost.

One of the routes lay across the glacier at Valdez. They came in over the terrible Edmonton Trail through Canada. It required two years for some of them to reach the Klondike by this route. Up the Kobuk River from Kotzebue Sound they struggled. The most popular route was up the Inside Passage through Southeastern Alaska to Dyea and Skagway, then over the Chilkoot and White Passes, and down the Yukon.

There are thousands of stories of individual hardship and adventure in the North. Perhaps the one of most interest here is the one that I know best: my father August Tobin's story.

My father and mother were married in a double wedding in 1894. The other couple was
my mother's brother Carl and his sweetheart,
Hilma. Both families were feeling great financial stress just when news of the tremendous
Klondike Gold Strike in the Yukon reached
the East Coast. The news jolted the whole
world. According to the newspapers, gold
could be just scooped up by anyone making
the treacherous trip to the frontier.

Like thousands of others, August and Carl
thought they just couldn't pass up the opportunity to get enough money to pay their debts
and maybe even be rich for the rest of their
lives. But how could they manage the trip?
How would their little families be cared for if
the fathers left for the gold fields?

Suddenly August had a solution! They'd toss a coin,
and the winner would go to Alaska and in a year or two
come back rich for both families. The loser would stay
behind and take care of the two families. What a plan!
August could hardly contain himself, yet he dared not tell
Emma right away. She'd try to talk him out of it. Carl
believed that it might work. In fact, he thought it HAD
to work.

Excitedly, like delinquent boys, they secretly made
plans. They couldn't go wrong, but they must act quickly
and get to the gold before others picked it up. Finally,
the two had hidden enough money for the four-day train
trip to Seattle. Luckily the railroad had been lowering

the forty-dollar price of a ticket to lure passengers aboard their trains.

Carl took a coin out of their stash in the red paint can. "What do you call it, Tobin?"

"Heads, I go. Tails, you go."

"All right! This is it!" Carl said with big grin. He flipped the shiny coin. It landed on the oilcloth-covered kitchen table then rolled off onto the floor. Both bent over, lost their balance, landed on their knees, and peered down to learn their fate.

"Heads it is! You lucky Swede!" Carl declared.

Finally, everything was in place for August to leave the next day, except now he'd have to tell Emma of their plan. How could he do it? Now he was realizing how hard it was going to be to not only tell his wife but to leave her and the kids too.

That night Emma, after nursing Florence, lay the baby down in the elegant, rose-mauled crib that sister Ottelia's employers had given her. Emma hoped that the fine bed with the good mattress would soothe her baby who tended to cry a lot. Sensing that August was unusually quiet, she wondered, *Is he thinking up some prank to play on me?* It was not unlike him to do so. *Maybe he's placed some surprise, like a bouquet of flowers, a mouse trap, or even an orange from the corner store between the covers on my side,* she mused. After checking between the sheets, she slipped into bed.

"My dearest, I have something very serious but exciting to tell you," August began.

"I knew you had something up your sleeve," Emma teased.

"I have been feeling so scared about our finances. It seems hopeless when the money doesn't come in to cover our bills. The people who promised to pay me for my work just can't do it. I owe so much to the paint company, I can hardly pass their store without feeling like the worst sinner in the world. The staff's glaring eyes feel like the devil himself is grinning eagerly at me."

I know the feeling, Emma clucked to herself.

"Pastor Simson used to tell us that in order to be saved we had to be good stewards and pay our debts."

"You think I don't know that?" Emma asked.

"Carl and I have been talking about what to do because he too, you know, is hurting real bad."

"I hear him complain about it every day."

"We came up with a fool-proof plan that will save both families," August said, trying to sound convincing. Emma rolled over to look August in the eyes.

"We can't let this opportunity pass us by," he said. "We've *got* to take advantage of it before it's too late. We decided we'll work together. It's fair, and both of us will come out rich."

"So we'll be rich when now we can't even pay our bills?" Emma shouted harshly.

"Tomorrow I'm leaving for Alaska to get rich for us and Carl's family. I'm joining the Klondike Gold Rush."

Emma bolted upright like a breaching whale. "*Du Vad?!* (You what?!)," she exploded in her first language.

After a mostly sleepless night, morning was announced by Florence's cry. Emma got up, and as she changed the diaper and sat down to nurse, she tried to convince herself that August was trying his best to

THE FLIP OF A COIN

support his family. She knew that when he and Carl got together they could come up with some wild ideas. Yet, they both were hard workers and good family men.

August had gone on that night to explain further. Emma would collect the eight hundred dollars owed him for painting and pay off the Fuller Paint Company. The remaining money that she'd send to August in Seattle would be plenty to cover his passage to Alaska, he'd assured her.

But wait a minute, she thought. *If August can't collect the money, how does he expect me to do it?*

The part of the plan that Carl would take care of their family might work, but he had barely enough money now to support his own family. She knew she could get along with Carl, but she barely knew Hilma. She wondered if Hilma knew about this yet. How would she feel about having three more people in their house?

After a satisfying nursing time, she finally came to the conclusion that August would be working harder than any gold seekers, and if any succeeded he'd be among them. *But why, oh, why didn't he tell me before now?* she thought bitterly.

That day in the late afternoon when the rest of the sibling families had gathered, August was ready for their farewell and good wishes. Several expressed envy because they were not going on this adventure too. But others whispered their concern to Emma that she'd have to be alone.

Neither August nor those left behind imagined the extreme hardships each would experience. They were all caught up in the excitement of easy wealth to be gotten in the Yukon that the newspapers told about. Emma didn't fear too much about the hardships she might experience in being left with all of the family responsibilities, because she had her sisters and brothers nearby to watch over her and the kids.

As soon as the train left, the family group rallied around Emma and the children. They offered to help move her household to brother Carl's. Emma was glad to have their help, because she realized that as she tried to move her belongings, they seemed twice their normal weight to her. Her mind was coming to grips with the situation, and she was weak with fear of the changes she'd have to make in order to fit in with Carl's wife and two kids. His place was no larger than the one she was leaving, and the lack of privacy was going to be a strain on all their relationships.

Yet, she tried to focus on her belief that August was trying his best to make their family happy and comfortable in the future. She worried a bit about her ability to collect the debt owed them, but August's positive attitude about it led her to believe she was capable of it.

* * * * *

Continuation of Tobin Talk

But the debtor went bankrupt. My father was stranded in Seattle without funds to go farther. My mother was unable to pay the Fuller Paint Company.

A romantic and adventurous painter, Ernest Morton, whom my parents had known in

Sweden and who had been working for my father in Boston, received an inheritance from Sweden. He decided to join my father. He went to Seattle, looked Dad up, and offered to pay my father's expenses to Alaska if he might join him as a partner.

Whalers at that time were losing money. The idea occurred to one vessel owner, and followed by others, to declare a stampede in the Kotzebue region, thus hoping to use their schooners for the transportation of passengers to that far distant point. The idea caught on, was successful, and whalers found it highly profitable, indeed, to carry gold seekers at two hundred dollars a trip to the mouth of the Kobuk River above the Arctic Circle. It needed but a few tales of great wealth found on beaches of that section to make men clamor for passage on the whalers.

Some whalers sold their ships outright. Such a man was the owner of the *Ellavina Johnson*, named after his eleventh child. He had had ten daughters. When the eleventh came, he ran out of names so he coined the name Ellavina for her.

Morton, Tobin, and four others bought the thirty-six-ton whaling schooner *Ellavina Johnson*, for twenty-seven hundred dollars. The group of six put the schooner in dry dock and

Morton and Tobin painted her. They were joined for the trip by a party of sixteen Scranton, Pennsylvania, farmers who had pooled all their resources for the trip to the gold fields.

In addition to being a house painter, my father was something of an artist. He drew sketches of all twenty-one of the men who made the trip with him on the *Ellavina*. I have them in an album.

None of the farmers knew anything about navigation—not even how to steer a rowboat. The only two in the party who had any previous seafaring experience were Harry Happel, a Gloucester fisherman, and my father. Dad had done some fishing out of Käringön, Sweden.

They made Happel captain and my father mate. They put aboard forty-eight tons of provisions and supplies, and sailed away April 16, 1898.

The ship was hit by storms on the Pacific and Gulf of Alaska. Happel proved a good seaman, but no navigator. They dubbed him "Columbus" because they claimed he tried to find a new route to the Orient.

He planned to touch in at Cook Inlet, but six weeks after leaving Seattle he was adrift and didn't know where they were. He was unable to steer.

The ship was becalmed after a storm. The captain and mate went to the stern of the ship to talk things over. While there, they looked down into the water. They saw a piece of drift following the ship as if attached to it.

"What is that?" asked my father.

"Just a piece of driftwood," said Columbus.

Tobin said, "It looks familiar. Let's have a look at it."

"My God! It's the rudder," exclaimed Columbus.

"I thought I had seen it before," said Tobin. "I painted it back in Seattle."

They drifted two days. By then they had rigged a jury-rudder from a part of the top of the mast when along came the Revenue Cutter *Bear*.

"Where are you going?" shouted Captain Tuttle of the *Bear*.

"We are looking for Cook Inlet," yelled Columbus.

"Then what in hell are you doing out here at Attu Island?"

Attu is the farthest west island in the Aleutian Chain, over a thousand miles from Cook Inlet.

The Cutter *Bear* towed them to Dutch Harbor where they made repairs.

The men on the *Ellavina Johnson* had heard the whalers tell about a big strike supposedly made on the beaches of Kotzebue Sound. "Prospectors were panning gold there like mad," the whalers lied.

They headed the ship across the Bering Sea toward Kotzebue, a thousand miles farther on. They had already sailed three thousand miles. This time Captain Columbus hugged the coast, keeping the shoreline in view while sailing through driftwood, so that he would not get lost again. Even so, he encountered the west end of St. Lawrence Island before reaching his objective at the east end.

The cook did not have much to do. Most of the passengers were sick whenever he prepared anything, most of it went overboard. Half the passengers were down in the hold praying. The others were swearing. They might just as well all have kept quiet. One group nullified the other.

Twenty days later they arrived off Kotzebue to find thirty-two small vessels and three big ships already there. Twenty-five hundred men were camped on the beaches.

There was no gold.

Of the twenty-two on the *Ellavina*, all but twelve headed south at once on other ships. Seven died of scurvy and other diseases the first year. Only three remained more than two years.

Dad and two others of the party, including Morton, decided to leave at once on foot for the headwaters of the Kobuk River. A big strike had been reported there. They started pulling a small boat loaded with supplies.

Many others had the same idea, but most soon turned back, including one of Dad's partners. But Tobin and Morton continued on, often wading up to their waists in the icy water. Twenty-nine men drowned, sixteen in one day.

Morton and Tobin lived off the country all the way. Luckily, there were salmon in the river, ptarmigan on the tundra, and berries on the banks of the river.

Few men have ever attempted the walk across the Arctic along the Kobuk as Morton and Tobin did that fall. Such a trip is almost unthinkable today, even with the help of airplanes. In 1952, for instance, the U.S. Army tried it with a group of soldiers to see if they could stand the hardship. Although planes dropped food and blankets along the way, the effort had to be abandoned less than half way up the river.

Morton and Tobin met Natives who had never seen a white man before.

Many of the early gold seekers carried articles they later found superfluous. They abandoned them en route. Some of these accouterments were really ridiculous.

My father told of one party of eighty aristocratic Englishmen, for instance, who each carried a chamber pot. The prospectors called them the "Chamber Pot Brigade," to use their most polite designation.

When they found how unnecessary their porcelain burdens were, the Englishmen presented the pots to the Indians along the way. For years thereafter, the Indians utilized them as tableware. I think they brought them out for potlatches and potluck dinners.

Morton decided to stop at Alatna, on the Alatna River, west of the Koyukuk. Dad got another partner and continued on. He went to Wiseman, on the Middle Fork of the Koyukuk River, seventy-five miles above the Arctic Circle. He stayed above the Arctic Circle in Alaska without going south of it longer than any other white man up to that time.

Chapter 3

August's Life Above the Arctic Circle

Shortly after August left, Florence got very sick. Dr. William Harvey, new to the community of Quincy, diagnosed her illness as pneumonia. He warned that she might be near death, so he lovingly treated her night and day, and along with her mother's care and medicine from the doctor, she recovered. That was a time Emma feared the most for the safety of the family without August. She thought that the cause of the illness was Florence's misery when sensing the turmoil of her father's departure.

Living with Carl and Hilma made caring for sick Florence doubly hard. Barely a year passed before living with the Ericksons became unbearable. Hilma's pregnancy signaled that it was time to make other arrangements.

When August got the news that his plans for the family to live with Carl and Hilma didn't work out, he was dismayed. He hoped the split had not been as severe as the one he'd heard about near Wiseman. In that case, two partners who shared a cabin became so incompatible that they decided to divide the cabin in half.

They drew a line on the floor marking off a section for each. Neither was to trespass onto the other's section. One of the ex-partners hung the clock in a place hidden from view on the other side of the cabin and declared it could not be moved. The ex-partner had to go outside to look in the window to find out the time.

The little Tobin family moved in with sister Ottelia and Knut. It was much more comfortable living with Emma's sister than with her sister-in-law. The sisters had similar ways of doing things. While August's life seemed full of adventure, the two children often suffered when they were teased because they had no father at home, but they kept up their pride and returned the teasing with tales of how they'd be rich when their dad returned.

Four years went by, and Emma's desire to be on her own became more and more intense. Finally, she told Ottelia and Knut that she'd found a tenement near sister Elin and Albin's.

"I've been feeling like I've been cramping your lifestyle all these four years," she told them. "You've been most generous, and I really appreciate all you've done in helping us. But August will be coming home soon, and we just need our own place."

"I've located a tenement a block from Albin's restaurant in South Boston. Emery's seven now and Albin said he could do some work for him. I know it would make him feel good to be contributing to our living. He can run errands for Albin."

The tenement building was one of many lined up near Broadway in South Boston. Tobin's two-room apartment on the third floor had no running water. The stove burned the wood carried up from the supply, stacked on the ground outside. Electricity hadn't reached the two-room rental yet. The odor from kerosene lamps lingered in the kids' memories on to adulthood.

Uncle Albin did have Emery make deliveries to and from his café. The little that he earned helped with the rent. Unfortunately, one day Emery tripped and fell on the cobblestone street, dropping and smashing every one of the dozen eggs he was carrying. He thought it was the end of the world because they were worth more than his weekly wage that he forfeited to pay for the eggs. He wondered how his mom would be able to buy enough groceries to last them that week. Fortunately that week a letter came from August with money enclosed.

When prospecting out of Wiseman, August occasionally was successful enough to have money to send home after paying his local bills. Those money-bearing letters, although few and very far between, always gave the whole family hope for their future. The letters instilled within the kids a curiosity about Alaska and a desire to experience the events their father wrote about. Stories like "He Robbed My Cache" were fun to hear when Emma read his letters to the children. They were glad to have such stories to entertain their friends.

He Robbed My Cache

Purgatory in Alaska? Yes, indeed, it is on the north bank of the Yukon River, twenty miles southwest of Beaver on the Yukon Flats.

I know the place well. I was a friend of the Yanert brothers who lived there. They were the cleverest men I've run across in the North. When discharged from the United States Navy, they hightailed it to the interior of Alaska and started a wood camp at the site they named Purgatory. The name was just one of many tokens of their humor.

Surprisingly, Bill was an accomplished poet and enjoyed composing rhymes during slack times. One of his poems, picturing life as he experienced it in each of the twelve months of the year, appeared in the *Alaska Weekly* newspaper in November in the 1920s. Describing December, Bill wrote:

The world's asleep 'neath a blanket white
A lonely owl hoots in the bush,
Above the stars and Northern Lights
And phantom voices whisper "Hush."
And a year has gone. I'll not meet it again.
The flight of years is not a joy to me.
How swift they come, and oh, how swift they go
But still I have my river—and am free!

In the summer the brothers operated a fish wheel that rotated with the river current scooping up fish, and in the winter they logged wood to sell to passing wood-burning steamers after the Yukon River broke up.

One of the brothers migrated south for a spell. The brother that remained was an artist, the best of wood carvers. He had made a clock entirely of wood that told perfect time. His sculptures of totem poles adorned the river bank. He was also a clever taxidermist. Stuffed birds and animals stood on a platform near the cabin door. A large stuffed bear seemed to growl at passersby. Inside the house he had a box full of wooden figures. I particularly remember an amusing little Black preacher, book in hand, with mouth wide open.

He did the carving when he had nothing else to do and would sit all day long with his feet dangling over the river bank, whittling away at something or other.

In spring before the river breakup, he became particularly lonesome for his brother. It was at this time that he started to work on the strange project I'm telling about, though for whose benefit no one knew, unless it was for the passengers on the river boats.

Whatever he did, he did well. First he made a large coffin, a very good coffin, and painted it black. Then to thaw the frozen ground, he built a fire and dug a hole six feet deep.

I don't know as I should tell you right now everything he put into the coffin, but for one thing, he dumped a lot of stones and gravel

into it, to make it about the heft of a man.
Then he sealed it, lowered it and covered it
with earth.

The grave, by the way, was right near the
wood pile on the side of the bank where all
passengers would see it when the steamers
stopped. On the top of the mound he erected
a wooden cross and carved HE ROBBED MY
CACHE.

The first steamer to come down the river from
Dawson landed in front of the wood pile. As
the boat tied up, the passengers went ashore
and one of the first things they saw, naturally, was the grave. They walked around it.
Looked at the words on the cross. Looked
at the lone wood chopper who, as usual, was
there to meet them, and whispered to each
other in awe-struck voices, "He killed a man!
Look, he killed a man!"

After loading all the wood needed, the steamer
continued down the river and stopped at Fort
Gibbon, the first village below. As the passengers began to intermingle with the inhabitants
of the miniature metropolis, the news spread
like a hail storm. "Fellow up the river killed a
man! Got him buried right outside his cabin!"

In a few days a steam launch drew up at Purgatory and out of it stepped a marshal and six

deputies. The wood chopper, as usual, was there to meet them.

The marshal stepped briskly to the grave. "See here, what does this mean?" he asked.

"Well, I found him robbing my cache."

"You're under arrest!" shouted the marshal. Then he ordered two of the deputies to guard the prisoner while he told the other four to dig. There was no lack of tools. As they dug, they made various remarks.

"By thunder, it's too bad."

"A man killing a guy for taking a little grub."

"A man caught robbing a cache ought to be killed."

"I wouldn't like to be him now."

Finally they reached the coffin and had a back-breaking time getting it up. At last they succeeded. Prying the lid off was another tough job. It had been screwed down careful-ly, so they had to borrow one of the prisoner's screwdrivers. At last, ready for almost any gruesome sight, they slowly lifted the cover. There on top of two hundred pounds of stone and gravel, carefully covered with a white sheet on a snow-white pillow, lay a little bird, the one called "Camp Robber" in Alaska, otherwise known as Canada Jay. In its claw was clutched a little bouquet of withered flowers.

The marshal grunted, gave the coffin a kick and exploded, "Turn the man loose. We're leaving." Then he stepped quietly onto the launch and drifted down the Yukon to the fort.

When details of their fool's errand leaked out, it was the joke of the far North. Whenever any of the fellows saw the marshal coming down the street, they would start talking and just about the time he was opposite them, they would say something like, "Yup, a fellow killed him. Too damned bad." Finally it penetrated far under his skin, so the marshal quit and beat it from the North.

The deputies heard about it for years afterward. They were still teasing some of the later deputies about it in when I left the area.

"Did you hear the news from Purgatory? Someone killed a fellow, caught him robbing a cache. Too damned bad!"

* * * * *

As August experienced disappointment after disappointment, without any lucrative claims, he felt obligated to tell the world how life really was for miners like himself. He spent winter hours writing articles for the

Swedish language newspaper *Westra Posten.* This one was published as he traveled toward Wiseman on his way to Dawson.

Westra Posten letter
September 8, 1899

We could trudge not more than three miles a day after which we had to set up our tent, rustle wood for fuel, and prepare our meal. On the steep grades we did not have the strength to pull the entire load, but had to make it on several relays. The temperature was between 45 and 73 degrees below zero. One of the men froze several toes and two fingers. We did not suffer much from the cold as long as we were moving about. It was much worse in the tent at night.

No one among us found gold. All illusions of glittering castles in the air tumbled. We had long since stopped figuring out how we were to haul out our riches.

As for our sick comrades, that was worse; 34 percent of the gold seekers in Beaver City suffered the excruciating pain of scurvy, the result of improper diet. Symptoms are exhaustion, stiffening of the limbs, and the skin of the legs taking on a dark, smoky color.

In the meantime, the terrible scourge was ravaging worse in Kobuk, which we had recently left, where four of our comrades of the *El-lavina Johnson*, including B. Benson died, as well as many others. In fact, in Beaver City, the majority of those were taken ill.

An inspection of our gold claims indicated all had the same results: nothing! For that reason, we decided to break away and try elsewhere.

On January 30, 1899, Morton and I, along with a third comrade by the name of D. Silena, left this terrible place and headed southward to try to reach Dawson. When we reached Arctic City, Morton decided to stay there, but I and one comrade continued the trip. After traveling fifty-eight miles farther south, we reached this place, Emma City, on the Koyukuk River. This "city" had five inhabitants whom, I fear, will vote for free silver at the next presidential election if legal free gold is not foreseen.

The Natives here are not much in evidence. There is not much wild game here, either. They say that an elk [moose] was shot here last year near Arctic City but this fact seems not to be particularly reliable, since such an animal has not been seen by any of us.

Bears could be hunted, but they spend most of their time in underground dens, hibernating.

I'll say in parenthesis that such animals seem to be suitable in this country, and it is regrettable that people up here are not equipped with the same instincts and capability.

Yesterday I saw what appeared to be wild geese gliding by, I understand that they were pilgrims like myself, winging their way south, and I only wish I had their inborn equipment to get away, as then I would have surely joined their company.

It has been figured out that about thirteen hundred people wintered on the Koyukuk, which included all the people between Beaver and Arctic City.

Everywhere we experienced a hearty welcome as everyone up here seems to live in harmony and accord. But this, of course, is natural in a place where there is neither gold nor women to quarrel over.

I was greatly astonished when I saw some newspaper clippings which somehow had found their way up here. They state that at several locations here there is staked hundreds of thousands of dollars worth of gold. In fact, they say no less than seven million dollars worth of this rich metal will be shipped out in the spring!

This newspaper exaggeration is the most flagrant I've ever read, and it is an inexcusable, deplorable tragedy that newspapers should lure its readers so outrageously.

The result of such colossal lies will be that more men will head this way to this miserable, forlorn, wild country to experience wretched hazards. Many people will be unconditionally attracted here—well, then, why not let them have their will?

On May 19 the ice broke on the river. We soon saw hundreds of homeward-bound gold seekers from our tent on the river bank. From the decks of the steamers, they shouted to us as they passed, "Hello!" and right afterwards, "Good-bye." From the tone of their good-byes was a definite determination that they had no intention of returning.

As for myself, I would truly never advise or dissuade anyone to come here and try his luck, because Alaska is large, very large, and it COULD happen that a man would strike it rich in this land where gold is found.

But this I want to say, you can't pick up gold from the ground with pinchers. One must freeze, and one must sweat before one brings up any gold if one is lucky enough to find it. Therefore, those who have their salt and bread and some security, better stay where they are. On the other hand, those who suffer much of strong gold fever better come here, for at least, they will find a cure.

Circumstances will probably demand that I stay yet another year, and in that case, you will eventually hear from me once more. Until then, I wish my friends among the paper's readers a hearty farewell—good-bye, until we meet again!

August Tobin

* * * *

The Tobin family, although they sometimes had very little to eat, could hardly imagine one experience August wrote about. Even though the end of the story repulsed them, they were proud that their dad would use the resources available to survive.

He wrote:

Mock Moose Meat

My partner John Schmitt and I were mushing on the way to Coldfoot when we were caught in a blizzard. Luckily, we were but a short distance from a cabin on Tramway Bar, a sandbar on the Koyukuk River, so we went there to hole up during the storm.

We had expected to be in Coldfoot that night so we had no food with us, but we found a sack of flour in the cabin. Cabins often are stocked with some grub that could be used in just such an emergency. While searching for more food, Schmitt climbed up the cache and found several chunks of what he recognized as moose meat under a tarpaulin. That was a real find, and Schmitt gleefully prepared a big pot of dumplings and stewed moose meat.

About the time we were ready to eat, Billy Glenn, also seeking shelter from the storm, burst through the door. Billy had no food either, so all three of us lived on the flour and meat found at the cabin. The storm lasted for days. Finally, the meat was almost gone. We had decided to stay in the cabin as long as the food lasted, then wallow through the snow to Coldfoot.

On the last day of our stay, Schmitt climbed up the cache to get the last piece of meat, but when he pulled the shank out from under the tarpaulin he was stunned at what he found. Coming into the cabin with the shank in front of him, he said, "Boys, did you know the moose in this section wear horse shoes?"

Right then, we no longer gloated over the tasty "moose" meat we had been enjoying!

We learned later that a mule belonging to the owners of the cabin had died. They had cut up the carcass for dog food.

While August was trudging up and down trails with heavy backpacks, Emma was often climbing up the steep ladder-like steps to their apartment, carrying wood for their stove in one arm and sometimes Florence under the other arm. Or often it was water she was carrying in one hand and a kerosene lamp in the other.

In order to make it work, Emma rented out their storage room and also, at times, the bedroom. Again her sewing skills were essential to their livelihood. She sewed often late into the night to finish a garment for a friend or relative. Emery, at eight years, was still working for his Uncle Albin and also selling newspapers to people on their way to work.

Fortunately, sister Elin and her husband, Albin's, restaurant and home were close, and Uncle Albin became a father figure to the children and trusted Emery to do many jobs in the café.

"Uncle Albin left me alone in the cafe for twenty minutes today!" Emery would boast some days.

Because the children mainly played with their Swedish cousins, their English was not always correct. One incident particularly embarrassed Florence when she was being taught to sew at school.

"What do you do next?" the teacher asked.

"I *wrinkle* the cloth."

There was a wave of giggling among the students. Straightening herself up and looking little Florence in the eye, the teacher stated sternly, "No, you *gather* it."

"Gather" in Swedish is *rynka*, which Florence thought was near enough to be "wrinkle."

Florence was so glad that day to see her mother waiting by the school gate to walk home with her and

Emery. Soon they were passing the alley beside the tenement.

Mrs. Schutte, who lived below the Tobins, was leaning out the window yelling at a man who appeared to be relieving himself.

"Ged oudda here! Don' you know kids play down dere?"

At the outdoor stairs, Emma stopped to pick up several pieces of their stored firewood for their stove, which provided them heat for the room as well as for cooking.

"*Mur*, (Mom) please carry me." Florence pleaded.

"No, you can climb all the stairs yourself now. You're a big girl. Don't forget to stop here and use the toilet."

"Hey, Mur, can I take my bath first tonight?" Emery begged.

"No, Emery, after you bathe the water's too dirty for Florence to use. She hardly gets the water dirty, you know. Boys are always dirtier than girls."

"Aw, please, Mur."

"Well, if you want to carry up two more buckets of water for her bath, you can go first. Be sure now to pick up all the wood you can carry, or your dinner will be cold tonight."

"Do you want me to bring up some kerosene?"

"No, we have enough for light tonight. That's nice you asked."

Reaching their third-floor two-room home, Emma began to put away the few groceries she'd bought, and then put some water on to boil for the potatoes. Ole, their boarder who rented out the storage room, would soon be there for dinner.

So with money from the rented bedroom and a storage room, Emma's sewing and money Emery earned, the little family survived between letters bearing bank certificates or gold nuggets from the far north.

This night there was not only a letter from August with some money but he'd also written a humorous story about folks who lived in Wiseman.

The Marriage of Brainy Smith
By August L. Tobin

The figures baffled me. There was one man only who could solve my mathematical problem—Brainy Smith. I shuffled through the snow to Brainy's cabin some fifty feet from my own.

Brainy glanced over the figures and quickly said, "You're right, Tobin. The assay office made a blooper."

Everyone knew Brainy. He unraveled many a problem. Prospectors swarmed from all directions to his trading post. Whatever they needed, from a button to a gold pan, they found in his log cabin department store in the center of Wiseman, 75 miles north of the Arctic Circle.

His real name was Frank Smith. He was ugly with a huge nose and a large mouth. Short and stooped-shouldered, he had an ungainly stride that could provoke laughter as his head bobbed up and down with each step he took. Under bushy, black eyebrows his small, brown eyes gleamed, making up for his bodily irregularities.

Everyone who knew Brainy counted him as a friend. He was always good-humored. His stock of witty stories never gave out.

Although the fates decreed that Brainy would go through life more or less a distorted figure, he was given more than his full measure of gray matter. He could add columns of figures in his head before there was time to write them down. Quick and keenly alert to everything around him, he had a memory and intelligence that never wavered. Few guessed he was illiterate.

When Smith first arrived at the Koyukuk in 1900, he worked at a sawmill operated by Gordon Bettles, "the father of the Koyukuk." Working with an Indian, Smith carried wood carefully, taking one board at a time, while the Indian loaded four or five pieces on his shoulders. Finally the Native thought it had gone too far: the white man was getting off too easily.

"You no strong. Me plenty strong," said the Indian, flexing his muscles.

"Yes, you plenty strong here," answered Smith, pointing to his arm, "but me plenty strong up here," pointing to his cranium.

On the next trip the Native supported but one piece of timber on his shoulder and, in explanation, pointed to his upper story with, "Me plenty strong up here, too!"

The sawmill owner overheard the exchange of remarks and said to Smith, "You're Brainy, all right." From that moment he was called "Brainy" by everyone who knew he'd padded his pay by prolonging the job.

Brainy was German with a drop or two of Jewish blood running through his veins. He was known from Seattle to Wiseman. He made a few trips to Seattle on business. Once seen, he was never forgotten.

In his younger days Brainy had been a rambler. At one time he managed a dance hall in Ceylon [now Sri Lanka]. He trekked the Sahara Desert, explored the Nile, lived in Death Valley. In 1890 he marched in Coxey's Army with the unemployed in Washington, D. C. He had been a hotel operator and had hoboed around the entire United States. He had made addresses at large gatherings: at a banquet arranged by the railroad king, James Hill, Brainy had made a stirring speech; it did not diminish his humbleness. He rode the rails on a score of trains. He boasted that he had been a professional tramp and pooh-poohed anyone who challenged such a doubtful profession.

With his hobo background, it was easy to understand how he stowed away in the cargo hold of a steamer bound for Skagway. In Alaska he had searched for gold from the Gulf of Alaska to the Arctic before settling down in the little mining village of Wiseman.

He became a successful merchant and post-master. He would meet a customer with a warm handshake and a hearty greeting, even when he suspected the visitor needed credit.

"Any mail for me?" a friend would shout, as he shook off the snow and stamped firmly on the floor. The customer would take the day off to read his letters, talk of this and that with the proprietor or others of that open country who converged on Brainy's trading post.

None of the fortune seekers who sat around the fire at Brainy's, one bitter cold winter evening in 1907, ever forgot that night. Their talk, as usual, covered the petty gossip of the village, news from back home, and the latest gold strikes. Brainy was in the midst of them. All were satisfied with the world, with them-selves. Contentment reigned.

Suddenly a man burst into the cabin, "I've news for you," he said. "A woman has come to the Koyukuk! She just arrived."

A hopeful murmur and thrill surged through the circle of bewhiskered men around the stove, as, truly, the news was startling. A woman in their midst was rare, indeed.

"If she is young and pretty, count me in as a contestant for her charms," grinned Brainy with a Don Juan roguishness. His expression lasted only long enough to finish his words.

All eyes turned and followed his to the outer door, which had swung wide open.

A woman of huge proportions filled the doorway. The men's shock was tremendous as, with quick comprehension, they grasped the meaning of her presence. Their chins fell on their chests, their hearts sank. The newcomer was indeed too voluminous to awaken any man's love. She was a colossus of female flesh and blood.

In her white fur coat she resembled a polar bear, except for the array of revolvers tucked around her belt, which disabused the observers of their mistaken impression and preconceived ideas of an angelic beauty. Her long, pointed nose and, indeed, her whole physiognomy was one of utter repugnance.

Her chest heaved like a billowy wave as with
mannish stride she stalked over to where
Brainy slouched. The look she gave the poor
storekeeper was enough to down an elephant.

"At last I've found you, you good-for-nothing
devil, and now I'll see that you never escape
again. The judge is with me. This very night
we will be married."

She shouted with such a blast of vehemence it
locked all ears and the very walls bulged out.

Brainy sprang up as though he had been bitten
by a snake and answered her just as courageous-
ly, but the Amazon did not lend an ear. She
bolted out as fast as she had blown in. All was
silent again. Indeed, the silence was so great,
had a nugget fallen on the floor the sound
would have made everyone jump with fright.

Brainy stood up. He was the object of everyone's gaze as he stood, stooped over. Suddenly
he straightened to his full height, lifted both
hands high into the smoke-filled room, and
burst out, "I'll give five thousand dollars to the
man who will take my place tonight!"

He looked around at the men. No one was in
the mood to accept the generous offer. Their
glances were directed to the door from whence
came terrible noises as the hippopotamus of a
woman thundered outside.

The hardy prospectors sat tense. The atmosphere congealed when Brainy strode out of the store into his own compartment, now that he realized no one would take his place at the side of the colossus. Did he intend to take his life? Such anxiety faded when he returned to the room clad in his heavy winter coat.

"I've never really been in love," he said. "I have avoided marriage, but since this Irish monster has searched me out here in the Koyukuk surely there can be no place on earth where I can hide from her. Therefore she will have her will.

"You and others have called me bright. My star is extinguished."

He was silent a moment, then set his lips firmly and continued. "For the friendship you have shown as always, your debts to me are now cancelled." He tore out the debtors' pages of his book and threw them into the fire. Then, with fallen head and humped back, he slipped out into the night.

In a short while a little group of men gathered in front of the trading post.

This was rare to see in daylight, and more so at night. A momentous outdoor spectacle was to take place. Frank Smith, alias Brainy, and Marie O'Hare were to become man and wife.

She had summoned Judge Howard to tie the knot. As usual the judge was three sheets to the wind.

The contracting parties stood together. I was selected as the best man, and the other prospectors became witnesses. The judge called for silence as he fumbled with a large book. He searched for the marriage ceremony. He tried to perform the ritual with the dignity of his office. He began rambling, stumbled, lost his place, started again. How the witnesses kept from laughing aloud surpasses the imagination.

Perhaps it was the first wedding the judge had performed. In any case, he had not memorized the ritual, and there was no hint as to what he searched for in the Sears Roebuck catalog, which had been hastily substituted for the Good Book.

The pint-sized stormy judge made up his own idea of a marriage rite, which turned out to be something like this: "From the world's extremity, with anxiety and disquietude, this young bride has braved the ocean, the ice and snow-covered mountains in order that she might up here above the Arctic Circle, meet her beloved, our good friend, Frank Smith, and become his mate till death do them part. Here under the glistening canopy of stars, in nature's large temple, I do tie Miss Marie O'Hare and Frank Smith so tight that Billy Glynn's horses can't pull them apart."

The ceremony over, amidst some joviality, the two were made one for this time and henceforth. Marie, now Mrs. Brainy Smith, sailed into the store, and at a safe distance behind the enormous hulk of a woman slouched Brainy, like a licked dog.

When Brainy opened his store the next day, his eyes were swollen. The bride's caresses had been violent. Though bowlegged and hunched, he was not a coward and feared nothing. In his younger days he had given many a big fellow his due, but on this wedding night he had been utterly defeated.

From that day forward Brainy was a changed man. With embarrassment and anger, he limped around the store. Seldom were Marie and Brainy seen together, but if they were, they were quarreling and each was ready to clutch at the other's throat.

Although Brainy was loose-mouthed in talking about the experiences of his younger days, not a word he divulged would enlighten anyone about how or where he had met Marie. He took the secret to his grave.

With his Irish lass, embittered Brainy left Alaska. He had at least a hundred thousand dollars with him. Thanks to fate, he soon became a widower in California, then doubled his money on his orange groves and other real estate. Brainy passed away, and just as the day is long, he had no enemy who might wish him united with Marie in the Everlasting.

Florence Thornton of Woodburn, Oregon, found the story "The Marriage of Brainy Smith" among papers belonging to her father, the late August L. Tobin, and translated it from the original Swedish. Tobin spent more than twenty years in the Koyukuk region and eighteen years in Southeast Alaska. Mrs. Thornton's brother, the late Emery F. Tobin, founded *The Alaska Sportsman*, forerunner of *Alaska* magazine. Translated from the Swedish by Florence Tobin Thornton.

Used with permission from *The Alaska Journal*, Bob Henning, publisher.

* * * * *

August kept trudging year after year far and wide in his search for the gold he knew was just around the next river bend. He was so determined that the holes he dug to bedrock, where the gold was usually found, were often more than a hundred feet deep, and they earned him the nickname "Deep Hole Tobin."

As the years passed, he outlasted many different partners, but it was easy for him to get new ones because of his hard work and jovial nature. He wrote home, affectionately, of one of his former partners:

Rose Hip Johnny
By August L. Tobin

News will sometimes carry one's thoughts far back to recall with vividness a chain of memories. A short time ago I heard of the passing of John Folger, and my thoughts brought back my remembrance of times with him. So Rose Hip Johnny has panned his last sandbar. He will mush no more.

Where e'er he now roams may roses have become rose hips and may his trail be paved with gold.

Johnny was a great trailbreaker, though very unassuming and consequently not heralded far and wide as others have been. He was a character unique, one of those real, hardy sourdough pioneers with whom one is proud to have been associated.

I have seen him toss his last can of milk to a fellow with, "Take this. I've lots of it."

However, we often find queer streaks in a good man.

He came to Alaska in '86 from Pittsburgh, Pennsylvania. His coal-black eyes and dusky skin led men to mistake him for a Native.

He had great strength of endurance. I never met his equal in all the years I spent in the North. In traveling, I am sure he had no peer. He never tired. On snowshoes, he cradle-walked like a Native. With a gun and ammunition, he could live off the country for months. He could squat down any place and call it home.

Once, in the spring of the year, while piloting a party from Fort Gibbons to the Koyukuk, he got off his course, and he and his party became completely lost in the wilds. One of the party died of hunger and hardship. The others barely came out with their lives. But not so Johnny—he arrived strong and hearty. He had subsisted on rose hips.

The three years I was his partner surely tested my mettle. The extent of ground in the Chandalar District that we covered was un-believable. Johnny was never quite satisfied unless he was "on the go." We would scarcely begin digging on some ground when he would indicate his restlessness. Greener fields afar were the words on his banner, as he recalled with enthusiasm some spot he had touched years ago.

Sand bar sniping was his specialty. I remem-ber him predicting the Iditarod strike which occurred many years later. He had panned

$200 at the point of a sand bar at the head of the Innoko River the year the steamer *Arctic* sank on the Yukon River.

I first met Johnny in the spring of 1900. He proposed that we boat up the North Fork of the Koyukuk River to prospect. We did and named creeks as we went along. We found surface prospects on nearly all of them but the ground was too deep and wet to locate anything of value. Fall approached before we came anywhere near the headwaters, so we decided to float back and return later on the ice. Our plan would then be to go clear to the head and over the divide to the Arctic slope, provided we did not locate pay dirt in the meantime.

Consequently, we made ready and started about the middle of October, "traveling light" with but one dog and sled apiece. Our equipment was merely a tent, some light bedding, a tin can stove, flour, rice, lard, tea, salt, a 30-30 rifle and a shotgun. Meat, all we needed, would be obtained by hunting, but blunder of blunders, we took along but one axe.

Johnny's dog, Jack, a Newfoundlander, was so old he was in continual misery. He was a good worker, but when he was pulling, he had a regularly occurring squeak coming from his lungs at every breath, very much like the sound of a frozen lung, the result of overwork. Johnny was very fond of his dog. When we started out he warned, "Now, where I sleep, my dog sleeps. I will divide my last biscuit with my dog."

"That's all right with me," I said. As for my own dog, Brownie, I believed he would be better off sleeping in a bed of boughs out in the open in order to become hardened to the cold weather.

It happened to be an off rabbit year, and we did not encounter any other game. We made fires and thawed the gravel on likely rims on various creeks but found very little color or gold. It snowed continuously and it stopped our progress, and the snow became a misty fog. We were pretty well up to head waters. The timber grew more scarce and scrubby. One day, towards quitting time, Johnny spied some tent poles resting up against a tree in a small timber patch.

"Look," he exclaimed, "and we thought we were the first white men up here! What do you say if we pull in and use those poles and this camping place."

We got the sleds up the bank. I began to un-lash our gear. Johnny pulled out the axe and started for the creek, intending to cut a hole.

The ice was about nine inches thick under a
foot of snow. When Johnny came back for a
bucket he reported that he had reached water.
The next time I heard his voice it was loud
and gave a rush of oaths.

"Tobin, I kicked the axe through the hole!" he
bellowed.

"That's a fine how do you do!"

We were hundreds of miles from nowhere
with five and six feet of snow behind us in an
arctic winter, without an axe to make a fire.
Anyone knows what that means. We were
in a terrible predicament, but we had to do
something.

After collecting our senses we looked around,
located the old tent spot, and I commenced to
shovel off the snow.

As I shoved my hand under boughs to shake
the snow off, I felt something underneath—a
small piece of wood. I pulled. It was heavy.
My heart throbbed faster—could it be? Pulling some more, out it came. I was electrified!
Yes, it was an axe. A brand new one! Probably,
my greatest discovery in the North.

A party of five men, so we learned later, had
made camp here a year previously over one
night. Dan Maddox, one of the party, had

been so attached to his axe, he had slept on top of it. Upon breaking camp the next morning he had forgotten it in the rush. That failure in his memory, if it didn't save our lives, at least kept us from experiencing a tremendous hardship.

We were very meat-hungry. We had been living on flapjacks and biscuits. Our flour was low. Next morning we started to retrace our steps. After a couple of days we found the snow was getting too deep. Our old tracks had become obliterated. Johnny's dog was heavy and would wallow through unless the trail had at least one night's crust. From then on we snowshoed ahead one day and returned to pull our sleds the distance the next.

One day, a week later, we were snowshoeing ahead when Johnny remarked, "Look up there. That is what looks to me to be a good sheep mountain. I think it would be a good idea if we snowshoed up to that nice timber in the middle of the creek yonder and tomorrow pitch our tent there."

I agreed. We had previously named the creek Ruby Creek. The following day we made camp.

The next morning Johnny advised, "Now I will go for sheep. Tobin, you better take the shotgun and go through the willows in the flat. Perhaps you can get a rabbit. I noticed some tracks as we came along."

There would be little use, I thought, to try for a rabbit, for even if there was one around he would hear me coming a mile off. However, after I cut down a tall, slender dry tree and placed it in front of the tent to be cut up for firewood in the afternoon, I started off. I feared it would be dark when I returned.

The short day had only four or five hours of daylight. After zigzagging along through the willows, it was time to turn back to be in camp by dusk. I did not see any rabbits and I am sure no rabbits saw me. Feeling extremely hungry and tired, it was tough sinking down a foot at each step with six-foot snow shoes. Walking was anything but easy.

Finally, I saw a light from our canvas tent. As I came close, my heart leaped with excitement, for in the light that streamed from the open flap of our tent, I could discern a half carcass of meat hanging in a tree over my dog Brownie's head! Quickly, I kicked off my snowshoes on our door-mat of boughs, and hurriedly I looked in the tent.

"Come right in," came Johnny's voice briskly. "You are just in time!"

As I stepped in, he lifted and uncovered a steaming pot of stew. I would not at that moment have changed my life with anyone. Meat-hungry as I was, I sat down to the meal with a mighty zest.

"Golly, man, but this is good," I said, as I reached for another helping and pierced the meat with my fork, "and it's tender, too. Must have been a young one."

I looked up at Johnny. He was eating with the apparent appetite of a famished man.

"So you do like it?"

"Fine. Never tasted better sheep meat. Now, if we only had some of your rose hip salad!" I joshed.

It was a meal to remember. The one thing that makes life a joy in the outdoor life of a prospector is just such a meal as this.

After lying back awhile against the roll of bedding enjoying a satisfying smoke, I made a break to cut the night wood. Not having a chopping block made my stick jump considerably. There was something peculiar at the top end of the log. My jumping stick had stirred up something. Stepping over to see better, I noticed patches of blood in the snow and with it, a kinky-haired jet-black skin. A black sheep?

"Johnny," I shouted, "have we eaten your dog?"

"Yes," he returned, "he was getting pretty old and useless. He wasn't good for anything else."

"Why, man!" I fired back at him. "You loved your dog. How could you do it?"

"Don't you see, Tobin, I raised that animal from a pup. He was always close to me. Now he is part of me," he said, as he patted his stomach. "If that isn't love, what is?"

"That beats hell, Johnny, are you crazy?"

"No. The meat tasted good. You said it did, didn't you?"

"Yes. It did taste good, but I'll be darned if I can keep it down now."

We didn't feast any more on the meat of poor Jack, and it surprised me that my dog would not touch the meat. It was not a case of "dog eat dog" with him.

The trip in itself was nothing unusual. Anyone who has tried hard for gold runs up against hardships as bad or worse. As for myself, this was only a tame imitation of what was to come in years to follow. I lost track of Folger as he left the Koyukuk for other parts of Alaska.

* * * * *

August's optimism seldom waned. He moved from one creek drainage to another, often naming them for his loved ones: Emma Creek, Emma Dome, Emery Creek, Florence Creek, Florence Creek Lake, Tobin Mountain, and Tobin Pass.

From time to time his diggings paid off, but his grubstake bills ate up the fruits of his labor. At other times nature herself intervened and wiped out all his hopes for riches. But there were other factors that seemed to be a threat to success; August related one of these.

A Double Crosser

When John J. Cooney and I were working at a certain creek, then unnamed, we considered what would be a good name for that creek. We expected to be rich—"kings" with everything in our power except crowns on our heads.

"Why not call it The Aristocracy?" I said. "Then we would be kings of the Aristocracy."

John heartily agreed, but that name was rejected by later prospectors in favor of *Tobin Creek*.

After Judge Howard and I struck a rich prospect on another part of the creek, taking out eight thousand dollars, I was panning gold further up stream when Jack McCord sauntered along. His eyes popped out when he noticed the rich residue.

"Will you let me try one? I'd like to know what it feels like to shake a treasure like that." McCord said.

"Sure," I replied. "You can do the next one that comes up."

"What do you think this is worth?" McCord inquired, as he finished shaking the pan.

"I don't know," I contemplated, "but I haven't panned one yet that's been under eight hundred dollars."

"Well, we'll say eight hundred then?" questioned McCord as he started to walk off, leaving the gold with me.

"Yes, about that," I nodded.

McCord then, straightaway went to Judge Howard's recording office. McCord bluntly told him he wanted to stake a certain claim on Tobin Creek. He didn't know that Judge Howard was my partner. We had staked the claim downstream from where I was working.

Howard was amazed. "Why you can't stake that; it's being worked."

"Yes," said McCord, "but it's not staked right."

"Have you panned any gold there?" Howard asked, expecting to catch him lacking one of the technical requirement needed before recording.

"Yes," McCord replied. "I just panned eight hundred dollars worth."

Judge Howard had no alternative. He had to let McCord register the claim.

McCord's scheme was to force five thousand dollars or more from us partners, for he knew he could lawfully stop all work. He knew we would pay all that and more rather than halt the successful panning.

But lo, the fates intervened. Then Mother Nature did a double-cross. The next day the rich mine filled with water and entirely closed all chances of mining as much as a teaspoon more of gold from the rich dirt.

* * * * *

After seventeen years in Alaska, August was mildly lucky and got enough money out of a claim near the Hammond River, not far from Wiseman, to pay off his debts and have enough leftover to pay for a trip to Boston. Friends urged him to go see his family. He needed little urging, in fact, but he realized it would be difficult to face friends and relatives after such a long absence with so little to show for his efforts. He thought if he mined the claim longer he'd have a greater fortune to show for his long absence. Longing to see his family won out, and he took off for home, planning to return for what he believed was a real fortune in this claim.

By riverboat from Bettles, he started south and arrived in Seattle a few weeks later without cash and with only a check. He knew no one who could identify him, but he bravely entered a bank that did business with Alaskans.

He handed the check to a teller, who flatly refused to cash it when August told him he didn't have anyone who could identify him. Then his artistic ability came to the rescue. He picked up an envelope and sketched a picture of hooked-nose Brainy Smith. Handing it to the teller he said, "Do you recognize this man? He's a friend of mine."

"Of course, that's Brainy Smith," he said as he handed August the money for the check.

Emma's hope that August was coming home "soon" had held for all those seventeen years. Then in that fall of 1915, Florence woke up to see her mom sitting on the edge of her bed.

"I have something to tell you."

Noticing a yellow paper in her mother's hand, Florence gave her a quizzical look.

"It's from your father."

"Is he all right?"

"He's in Chicago today. He'll be here tomorrow!"

Snatching the telegram, Florence read, "Will arrive South Station Boston at eleven a.m. Sunday."

Florence could say no more. Her voice was gone. Her lips quivered. She choked as tears fell. Shaking like she was having a convulsion, she threw her arms around her mother and cried.

"I was afraid you'd take the news like this. I wanted to break it to you gently."

"Does Emery know?"

"No, Emery left for work two hours ago and the telegram just arrived."

Emma appeared calm as she went about her work the rest of the day, but what was she thinking?

Florence had twenty-four hours to compose herself, but her thoughts continued racing through her head. *Would her* fahrr *(father) like her? Would they really be rich now?*

Emma sent word to her siblings about August's arrival time. Looking like a flock of chickens expecting to be fed, they were all there to meet the train. Who would spot him first? Would any of them recognize him after all these years?

"I see him!" Emma shouted. He's the one wearing that leather beaded jacket, and he has a mustache!"

August muscled his way toward the little group as they moved excitedly to him. Then the hugs and kisses began and continued until August got confused about who some of the family members were. After all, not all had been married when he left. They had to stop and introduce him to their spouses and children born after he'd left.

"Let's all go down to my place," Albin invited.

There in Albin's South Boston restaurant they gathered around the long tables. They were all ears to hear everything August had to offer about his adventures in Alaska.

August opened one of his bags and pulled out the sample nugget he'd chosen to impress them with. He

80

handed it to Albin and watched for his surprise when the nugget, weighing six ounces, was so heavy that his hand dropped from its weight.

Later, August took Carl aside and gave him what he thought was fair for having his family stay with him. Carl was not pleased.

"The agreement was that we'd split the treasure equally, August. Where's the rest of my share? I've got eight kids to support!"

"Listen! Emma and the kids stayed only a few months with you, not the seventeen years I was gone! What little more that I have stays with me."

The little he kept for himself was to pay the Fuller Paint Company the eight hundred dollar bill he'd owed when he left, save some for his family, and just enough more to pay his way back to Wiseman to the claim that finally promised a real fortune. He held on to the hope that he would come back rich if he could work that claim for just a little longer.

For several months, the Tobins lived a somewhat normal life together in the little tenement. Now August carried the supplies up the steep stairs. After the children were in bed, August and Emma had long conversations about their future. Then it was time, August thought, to make that trip back and claim the riches he knew were waiting for him on his Emery Creek claim. Emma knew that he planned to return to Alaska and dreaded the day when he would again leave for "maybe a year or two."

August promised, "When I return, we'll buy just the house you dream of. There's so much gold down that hole, I'll scoop up enough for a house in no time."

Emma could hardly believe what he told her; yet he had such a convincing way that she let herself hope that it would be true.

The trip back to his claim was much easier than seventeen years earlier when he hardly knew how or when or where he was going. Traders in the Interior had been pleading for improved transportation, which would make their prices compete with those sold on the coast. Now more and more steamships were pushing their way up the navigable rivers, giving travelers actual time schedules as they headed for their destinations. Bettles was the end of the line for steamers. From there, depending on the season, August could take a dog team or pole boat the rest of the way to Wiseman.

Arriving in the little town of Wiseman that had a collection of most of the two hundred fifty inhabitants of the area, he was the center of a mini-homecoming when his old pals greeted him warmly and walked him to his cabin, which was just as he'd left it.

August lost no time in getting his mining gear together and hauling it up to Emery Creek. He was elated that his claim yielded rich pans. *Yes, I'm going to be a rich man!*

News of his good fortune spread, and he was invited to play poker with the guys one night. Remembering Pastor Simson's tirades about the evils of gambling and playing cards, August was slow to accept.

"Come on, Tobin, you're a rich man now!" they teased.

I guess I can afford to lose a few nuggets, and who knows, maybe I'll be the winner!

THE FLIP OF A COIN

But his luck didn't hold out and he lost three hundred dollars. He was so mad at himself that he took a lantern and went down into the deep shaft he'd dug. Picking up a couple of floor boards, he uncovered a mini-mine of sizable nuggets—five hundred dollars' worth. *My, god! That's the first time I've ever come out ahead after playing poker!*

The next day he went confidently back to the bonanza. He began climbing down the shaft toward the treasure he knew was there, but water twenty feet deep had flooded the claim. He had no means of siphoning it out. Again his dreams were shattered.

Going back to his cabin he was, this time, completely discouraged. The price of grubstakes had gone sky high and the price of gold remained the same. With the wonderful memories of being with his family in Boston, he decided to return home without achieving his dream of getting rich.

This time, because he'd incurred some debt for the grubstake he needed, he didn't have the price of a return ticket on a river steamer. He walked two hundred miles and accepted free rides whenever offered. When he was far enough south, he used the roadbed of the railroad which was being built between Seward and Fairbanks. Coming upon a railroad crew at lunchtime, he asked if they might share a sandwich with him. He was used to the helpfulness of everyone in the north who shared with any stranger who came along.

The answer, "Naw, move on. We ain't got nothing extra" took him aback and he felt even more of a failure. *Do I appear to be just a lazy bum?*

In Seward he was lucky to get a job stevedoring that paid enough for a steerage ticket as far as Ketchikan. While waiting for the next ship going south, he met a well-dressed man hungry for stories of the Great North. August learned that he was a millionaire from New York and entertained him with tales of good fortune until late that night. As they parted, the man said he wished he could spend more time listening to the stories of instant millionaires being made in the gold fields, but he was leaving in a few hours on the next steamship. The friend believed August had been one of the lucky ones to take out a fortune. August, too ashamed to let him know he was traveling the poor man's way (steerage), didn't mention that he also was leaving on that ship.

In order to avoid being seen by his millionaire friend when he went on down to the steerage section, August went aboard hours ahead of their departure time, found his bunk and slept until the ship's cast-off whistle blew as it left the dock.

August woke and looked out at others just getting settled. Lo and behold, there was his friend stashing his luggage in a steerage space. Just then their eye met. "Hey, Tobin, too bad. I see you couldn't get a first-class reservation either when they were sold out."

"No, tough luck. I guess we'll have to put up with it. I'm glad we're together, anyhow."

There was no end to the stories August related to the fascinated man from New York. All the way to Ketchikan, the unlucky Swede told of huge fortunes earned from the hard work of others in mining.

August Tobin grew up in Käringön, Sweden, a fishing village built on bedrock that barely breaks the surface of the North Sea.

Pastor Simson, minister of the church at Käringön for over fifty years, ruled the congregation with an iron hand.

The Käringön church appears much the same today as when August Tobin attended it over 125 years ago.

Mansion on estate where Emma Erickson Tobin grew up, Oaxon, Sweden, has most recently been a five-star restaurant.

86

Register of the schooner Ellavina Johnson, *Harry Happel
in charge, sailing for Unalaska … from Port Townsend,
Washington, April 18, 1898.*

*Ever practicing his
artistic skills, August
Tobin sketched Lewis
Bortha, a passenger
on the* Ellavina John-
son *on their way to
Kotzebue, Alaska.*

Ernest Morton, whom August Tobin knew in Sweden, partnered with him as they prospected in the Arctic.

Roadhouse in Wiseman, Alaska, as it appeared in 1955.

In 1954 Florence Tobin Thornton, center, visits with Wiseman residents from left: Bob Jones, Jess Allen, Bill Kirkpatrick, Ken Harvey.

Florence, Emma, and Emery Tobin, Quincy, Massachusetts, five years after their father, August, left for Alaska.

Tobin Pass, Wiseman District, was named for August Tobin.

Florence and Emery Tobin as teenagers in Quincy when their father was in Alaska.

Emma and August Tobin together in Boston on his return visit home after seventeen years in Alaska.

Part Two

Chapter 4

After Twenty-Two Years,
Son Meets August in Ketchikan

August's son, Emery, returning from WWI duty in France, was inspired to write to his dad in Ketchikan, where he was working to accumulate enough money for the rest of the trip to Boston. Seeking his own Alaska adventure, Emery asked his dad to remain in Ketchikan so he could meet him there. He planned to stay about a year and then they would return to Massachusetts together. Since August was stuck there without money to proceed East, it was no problem to remain and welcome his son.

Ketchikan was a bustling little town where the fishing industry was just being developed. Emery got work as a bookkeeper for the New England Fish Company (NEFCO). His dad, too, got work with the company. He was hired first to paint the new houses the company was building for its employees, and then as the engineer who kept the fish cold storage plant as cold as the twenty-two arctic winters he'd experienced. NEFCO allowed them to pitch a wall tent on its property. Emery had never been as content as when he lay snug on his bunk with the unending rain drops sealing him inside his dry environment. At last he had a dad to share his life with. His curiosity about his father's life in the Arctic never waned.

"Dad, when you were up north searching for gold, did you ever have any near-death experiences? I mean did you ever think that you'd never see us again?"

In the Grip of a Yukon Breakup

Well, son, in the twenty-two years I fought the elements above the Arctic Circle, constantly in search of gold, I mushed on the trail at 60 below, I dug holes three hundred feet into Mother earth, and I enjoyed the warmth of the Alaska mid-summer. But the adventure of all these years that burns most clearly and sears my memory most deeply is my adventure in the roaring waters of the mighty Yukon River during a spring breakup.

This is the story that the millionaire in Seward was most fascinated by, so he had me tell it again and again to various groups he gathered while we were coming down here to Ketchikan. So I have it well-polished as a spellbinding tale.

In 1918 I was working for a grubstake at Beaver on the north side of the Yukon. Frank Yasuda, a Japanese trader, had offered me a winter outfit in exchange for cutting wood to be piled on the bank of the Yukon for sale to riverboats for fuel.

I had been working for five days when the river broke. What a tremendous sight! Great blocks of ice, slush, trees, and jumbled piles of wood, such as I was cutting, churned by. Occasionally a rowboat and the results of many a prospector's winter work went down the stream in the rumble of the river.

For two more days I sawed and cut wood on the bank. The banks in nearly all other places were high from the roaring stream, and the river was cutting under them here and there, eventually toppling thousands of yards of undercut bank into the river, taking with it trees and whatever nature or man might have placed thereon.

Frank Yasuda's store was about a hundred yards back from the bank. There was no danger of the river cutting in on me where I cut wood. After two days the river became more calm. After the first rush, the ice and flotsam floated by more lazily. Slush still continued to come, and great cakes of ice that once had been the solid surface of the river, five- and six-feet thick, drifted by.

On the third day George, a stuttering trapper, good friend of Frank Yasuda came to pass the time of day with me as I sawed and split. The movement of the river had become monotonous; we hardly paid any attention to it.

Then, suddenly, like a shot out of a cannon—
a great force of water came rushing down, like
the Yukon when she first broke three days ago.
Great cakes of ice tumbling and grinding and
great trees rushed by, rolling like clowns on
the circus ring.

"Gawd—what's this?" I yelled at George.

"The P-p-p-porcupine h-has b-b-b-broke," he
stuttered.

That was it: the mighty Porcupine River,
tributary of the Yukon, had released her winter store of ice and was on rampage, pouring
her age-old pines and sturdy cottonwoods and
ice and slush into the main artery.

We watched, fascinated. Suddenly, 'way up the
river, coming our way, I saw the bulky form of
a brand new trader's scow, with something piled
high in the center, covered with new canvas.

"Oh, George," I yelled at him above the roar
of the river, "Look! There's a prize for you!"

"A scow . . . maybe furs . . . thousands of
dollars worth! Oh, George," I cried, and I
jumped up and down with impatience at such
wealth coming our way, yet out of reach.

George was immediately excited. Trapper
instinct, probably, fascinated by the results of
someone's winter labor rushing down the stream

this way, obtainable now, except for the grip of the Yukon, with probably a few hours labor.

"Ohhhhh!" stuttered George. "What y-y-you say we g-g-g-going g-g-g-getting it?"

"Can't, George . . . no . . . use . . . got no boat," said I, getting more excited, too.

"I g-g-g-going g-g-g-getting one. F-f-f-frank got one. I g-g-g-get it." And he was off for the store like a streak.

The temptation was too great. I streaked after him, and together we carried the boat from the rear of the store building to the bank of the river as the scow came nearer and nearer.

We shoved the boat, a clinker-built three-seater, into the stream. As we pushed it in, I noticed a tiny trickle coming in from between the lower seams.

Excited, lest the scow get past us, I shouted at George, "Get something to bail with . . . quick!"

George rushed away . . . was gone only a minute, and was back to the boat. We were off. The river swung the boat into the stream. I took the oars. George was at the bow. I could not see him. I was occupied in maneuvering the boat. We were in deep and dangerous water now. Suddenly it dawned on my consciousness that the boat was filling with water! Gosh, what fools we were! The boat hadn't been used for years. Our weight pressed the water through the openings between the seams. Before I had the oars in the locks, my ankles were soaked.

"Bail, bail, George, for all you're worth!" I screamed, trying to head the filling boat out into the current. If we didn't get out, we were bound to strike the bank, just below where the water was cutting under it deeper and deeper.

"I b-b-b-bailing all right," I heard George say, then I turned to look. Bailing! How could he be bailing with the water coming in this way? The water was crawling up to my knees!

What I saw struck me dumb. George was bailing against the in-rushing stream with a tiny Eagle milk can.

It was too late to complain. Our boat was quickly getting into the jumble of ice cake and flotsam and jetsam, and the scow was nearly abreast of us twenty feet away! We were going down, down, down. Talk about a sinking feeling! Nothing to grasp onto. I had never been in such a situation except in a nightmare.

"Can you swim?" I next shouted at the laboring George, who still worked away with the milk can.

100

"N-n-n-no, I no swim," came the answer, as I gave up the hopeless task of pulling at the oars, with the water nearly up to the locks.

"Then stick to the boat," I yelled. "I'm off!"

Into the mass of ice and slush I went. Strange to say, I did not immediately feel cold, in the excitement. It was impossible to swim, though. The ice and slush swept around my arms. It was all I could do to keep myself afloat. For how long, I had no idea.

Bewildered, I soon found myself half mile downstream. I was getting numb, but had been able to keep my head above the mass of surging ice. Any minute my life might be blasted out between the grinding cakes. I tried to take stock. Think what to do. My mind was distracted by a sudden splash ahead. A great piece of the bank had fallen into the river five hundred feet ahead of me. All the bank had not gone. The water surged under the rest of the undercut. I was headed for the place where the bank fell in. If I went under the bank, I could be a goner in no time. There would be no chance to breathe in that caldron of icy, boiling water under the bank.

Suddenly, I saw a straw of hope! As the uproar caused by the giant splash of the bank falling in the river cleared away, I saw,

101

standing upright still, one of the trees which had been standing on the bank but now was standing, nearly as erectly, in the river where the bank had fallen. The mud and roots anchored at the bottom held it up in spite of the pull of the river rushing seven or more miles an hour past its trunk and branches.

I was headed for that tree. Could I make it? With feeble efforts I tried to direct my body toward it. I made infinitesimal progress in the direction, but if I did not hit that tree and climb upon it, my last chance would be gone. I would be carried under that bank just ahead. It would be like going into a grinding tunnel whirling with water, a most horrible death!

I somehow managed to take another deep breath as the Yukon rushed me on. I had been through many narrow escapes, and fate had often miraculously pulled me through. I recall the time I just crawled out from under the prospect drift, and the bucket crashing down on me, only to be caught by the steam pipes five feet above me. Could my lucky fate save me now? The wheel of fortune was turning, turning, would it stop at red or black?

More ice cakes brushed against me, almost shoving me away from the direction I hoped to take, like giant animals . . . brushing me

away from hope, to fate. Would I reach it?
I was nearly stiff with numbness. But, excitement somehow seemed to keep my feeble
muscle awake. Ten feet . . . five feet . . . one
foot . . . The tree! I reached out, and oh, oh,
oh! I grasped a branch. What a relief! I clung
on for a second. Then, with the current almost pushing me up, I managed to slowly pull
myself up to the lowest branches and hugged
the tree, standing there at last, out of the wet,
with the steep bank ten feet to the right of me
and twelve feet above me.

I looked back for George. *Poor George!* I
thought, though far from saved myself.
Downriver I saw a black speck. It was George,
still clinging to the boat. All I saw was the
back of his head. "Too bad," I murmured.
"Good-bye, George."

I looked at the bank. I felt the tree swaying
gently, like in a dull wind. Ten feet from safety, but it might as well have been miles, so far
as I was concerned. The water rushed between
me and the bank with exasperating swiftness.
And how long would the tree stand, thus erect
in the swirling stream? I almost felt as if I
were no nearer safety than while in the water.

"Help! Help!" I yelled at the top of my voice.
But who was there to help me here, and who
even to hear my feeble voice against the

thunder of the river? I was a mile from Frank
Yasuda's store and a mile from Beaver, where lived
the scanty population of seven carefree souls.

"Help! Help!" I yelled again, and it seemed
as if the mighty river, holding me in its vise-
like grip was mocking me and laughing, till it
would at last have done with fooling with me
and draw me down to its heaving bosom that
had been the grave of so many other wretched
souls. Then . . . I heard a slow-moving, feeble
voice from the bank. I turned! I looked! Up
there . . . on the bank . . . looking down . . .
was a man! Frank Arnold!

Arnold was slow, but he was like an angel
from the sky to me. Out of all that Alaska
wilderness, where did Arnold come from
then? Arnold drawled, but his voice sounded
sweet to me.

"Hey, there," he said. "How . . . did . . .
you . . . get . . . down . . . there?"

"I swam for it, Arnold. Quick, help me,
quick! Fall a tree. Point it upstream. The top
will float down and hit this one. And for
God's sake, be quick!"

Arnold's form slowly disappeared from above
me. I saw him turn, and the last I saw of him
for half an hour was the back of his head as he
walked away.

It seemed hours till he returned. The tree held, but I expected at any minute to be tumbled into the stream as the river tore at its roots. I learned later that the river tearing at the bank was Arnold's reason for being at the particular spot at that particular time. He also had piled up cords of wood to sell to passing steamboats and was hauling the wood back out of the reach of the hungry river when he looked over to see the damage the last cave-in had wrought and saw me.

Arnold came with a long, dry pole, all right, but after he had it in position, and the top had swished down the river at me, I saw that I must have another to climb ashore, otherwise, the small one, rolling around with me, would thrust me into the river's jaws again.

Again I waited, as the slow-moving Arnold "hurried" off to fell another tree. I was thoroughly chilled to the bone, and was cold as the ice in the river below me. I was stiff and cold as an iceberg. Though benumbed and half dead, I managed to hang on, somehow, to the tree and wait for Arnold. At last he came with the other tree! I must say that he was efficient, if slow, and he again laid the second tree precisely where I would have it. Even slower than the lumbering Arnold, I laboriously climbed ashore.

Arnold stood smiling as, heavy as lead and aching with numbness, I stood up on the bank. "Thanks, old life-saver," I shivered, and limbering up, ran as fast as I could for my cabin at Beaver.

The fire was not quite out in my stove. I was able somehow to get it blazing to thaw myself out, and three hours later I sat by my stove, a towel wrapped tightly about my bursting head. I was thinking, disconnectedly, of poor George. Too bad George had to die in that cold water! And all for nothing! George was a good little scout. We had been thoughtless. Reckless. We might have known a tragedy would result.

Through my splitting headache, I heard someone at the door. As I looked up, there he was—George and his friend, Frank Yasuda.

"H-h-h-hello, h-h-h-h-here I be."

"W-w-w-what?" I exclaimed, stuttering, too. "H-h--how in the world did you get out?"

"O-o-o-oh! I-I-I-I g-g-g-etting out all right. I hold on to the boat and oar. I-I-I-I- g-g-g-g-etting oar on two blocks ice, c-c-c-c-limbing out on bank, then I-I-I t-t-t-take o-o-oar and push block of ice like skull b-b-b-b-oat and p-p-p-p-ush him to shore."

Ever afterwards, whenever I met that plucky
Japanese, I would exclaim, good-naturedly,
"Oh, George . . . look, there's a big scow coming
down the river . . . hurry up . . . let's go get it!"

His inevitable reply would be, "N-n-n-no,
thank you v-v-v-elly much, please. I no want
um scow n-n-n-no more. Thank you v-v-v-v-
v-elly v-v-v-v-elly much."

"Wow! I had no idea you'd come so close to your
last day on earth! We had it tough in Boston, but we
weren't in that kind of danger," Emery said in astonish-
ment. "I think you've had more than your share of good
luck. Maybe it's because you've been such a hard worker
and always tried to do what's right. Have you ever heard
of Horatio Alger?
"No, why?"
"Well, I've been reading a lot of his stories, and I
think he's got it right. All his characters succeed under
the most awful conditions, because they've been hard
workers who were always honest, plus they had a lot of
determination and courage. I think they could be true-
life stories, and that's the way I want to live my life. Your
experiences prove to me that such a philosophy works.
The success part may not be the success you're looking
for but some kind of success that brings us all happiness."
"Well, I don't know. It just comes naturally. As for
success . . . I'm still alive. I guess that's success."
"Yeah, we may not be rich with money, but we sure
have it swell here with good jobs and a wonderful, cozy place
to live," Emery said, as he moved over to his typewriter.

Emery wrote almost-daily letters to his mom and sister in Boston. They were filled with descriptions of his outdoor activities. He even turned into an adventure story his own near-death experience of getting lost while hunting that was published in several Eastern newspapers. Every weekend this city-bred man went on a fishing-, hiking-, or hunting trip. His love for the outdoors was bound to be a driving force in his decisions for his future.

* * * * *

In two years August and Emery saved enough money to send for Emma and Florence. They were enthralled by Emery's glowing reports of the work opportunities the growing town offered, and the exciting outdoor adventures one could experience in the forests and on ocean excursions. By the time the men sent money for their tickets, NEFCO had finished building houses for their employees. The tent had been an adventure, but moving into a real house was like actually striking it rich on the gold fields. Although they wouldn't own the home, August's promise to Emma of a house was materializing. The rent was minimal and the utilities were free! Their experiences were turning into a Horatio Alger story.

It was fairly easy for Emma to accept the ticket to Ketchikan, but for Florence it was a difficult decision. Her boyfriend had recently moved to Florida, and he was encouraging her to follow him. Besides, she had secured quite a good job with a bank in Boston. So should she stay with "the bird in hand," go south or go north? Emery assured her that she could find employment with one of the government agencies in Ketchikan at much more pay than what she was getting in Boston.

So both women got on the trains that would take them across Canada to Vancouver, B.C., where they boarded a ship for the two-day cruise to Ketchikan. The NEFCO house that was ready for them seemed as elegant as the mansion on the estate where Emma had lived as a child in Oaxen, Sweden. It had two bedrooms, a living room, dining area, a porch, running water, a telephone, and electric heat and lights from NEFCO's power plant and all on one floor!

Adjusting to August's graveyard shift at the cold storage plant was a problem. He was used to the quiet of the arctic wilderness when he slept. The problem was solved by building a cabin, named "Kamp Kliff" on the hill behind their home where he could sleep undisturbed.

With abundant energy and enthusiasm from their comfortable living, the whole family pitched in to build a tennis court for all the neighborhood to use. First the natural growth of trees and brush had to be removed. Then the surface needed leveling. They finished it by spreading several loads of gravel on top. A chicken-wire fence kept the tennis balls from being lost in the uncleared muskeg around the court. The work had all been done without the benefit of powered machinery.

For further entertainment, Emery and Florence explored the trails leading to mountain tops, lakes, and streams. It was all so exciting for them to be together in a place of much adventure. Emery helped establish a Boy Scout troop and Rotary Club. Florence got involved in music and theatre groups. Soon thoughts of her Florida beaux faded when many young men became interested in this talented young woman. She secured a job with the Lighthouse Service that put her in touch with many lonely lighthouse keepers, when they returned to town after months of solitary lighthouse living. Her social calendar was as full as a Hollywood actress'.

Having experienced their hard life in Massachusetts without her father, Florence was determined not to marry a man who would be gone for months at a time. She was over forty years old when Laurence Thornton came into her life. He was a gold miner too, and would be gone to his claim beneath Chickamin Glacier, near the Canadian border northeast of Ketchikan for many months. Finally, Florence secured him a job at the Lighthouse Service dock, and he kept the job for a year making him eligible, in Florence's mind, for marriage. They were happily married for five years before he died suddenly of a heart attack.

Emma was content to manage the household, but Emery and Florence were eager to climb three-thousand-foot Deer Mountain behind Ketchikan or walk to Ketchikan Lake where the city's water that generated electric power originated. They went on small-boat trips for picnics on distant beaches, where ruins of Native villages with rotting totems could be explored.

The family's dinnertime main course was free because of fishing for salmon, cod, or halibut in the salt water or trout from lakes and streams. They dug squirting clams at low tide. The most coveted delicacy was halibut cheeks, available when the halibut boats were unloading, and anyone could cut them from the huge flat fish before the unmarketable heads were disposed of.

To vary their diet even more, Emma was able to get the men to build a hen house and chicken yard so she could raise a dozen or more chickens to provide eggs and meat. Their garden produced all the vegetables they could eat and share with neighbors. Compared to their hard lives in Massachusetts and the Arctic, the family thought they were among the luckiest people on the planet. They all felt rich at last.

Chapter 5

Roots Are Planted in Ketchikan

Meeting the steamships that passed through Ketchikan was a common pastime. The passengers were interesting to watch, and sometimes there was a VIP aboard, because the steamships were the only way to get to Alaska.

"Say, Emery, what do you say we meet the next ship?" asked Alma Todd, NEFCO secretary to superintendent Harry Noonan. "I met a friend of my sister's in Seattle when I was South. I think you ought to meet her. She's going up to Seldovia to teach school. Her name is Clara. Clara Willard."

"Sounds good to me, Alma. What day does she arrive? But where in the world is Seldovia?"

"Saturday morning about ten. I'll meet you on the dock. Seldovia is south of Homer on the Kenai Peninsula. Everybody fishes there, and they're really doing well."

And so it was that the two friends stood on the Alaska Steamship dock that misty Saturday morning, looking down Tongass Narrows for the first glimpse of the steamship from Seattle. Soon she was in sight, and within the next hour they were greeting a surprised Clara Willard.

At the end of the gangplank Clara exclaimed, "Alma! It's so good to have you here! You make me feel comfortable knowing I have a friend in Alaska."

"Well, Clara, I want you to meet my friend, Emery Tobin. He works with me at New England Fish Company."

Emery's heart was racing, but he managed to say, "How do you do? I'm so glad to meet you. We're wondering, since your boat isn't leaving for six hours, if you'd like to see the sights around here. I have some time off and I'd like to show you the town. It means we'll be doing quite a bit of walking, though."

Emery held his breath. Would this charming beauty with dark brown eyes accept?

"I'd love to. I was wondering what I'd do while the ship is docked."

Alma said, "If you'll excuse me, I promised I'd meet Fair Snodderly for coffee at the Blue Fox. You're in good hands, Clara. And Emery, I'm sure she's used to long walks."

When it was almost time for the ship to leave, Emery and Clara were rushing back to the dock, barely reaching the ship before the cast-off whistle blew.

It had been love at first sight. Emery and Clara walked several miles to Emery's favorite spots.

As they had walked downtown on the boardwalk, the traffic thumping along on loosened planks almost drowned their conversation, but they soon reached the narrow gravel street along Ketchikan Creek. They'd stopped for awhile to watch the salmon jumping the falls, then went on along the creek to the newly built Ketchikan

Park where salmon were spawning. A little further, Emery pointed out the Deer Mountain Trailhead where he often began the three thousand-foot climb to the top. "I wish we could climb Deer Mountain together today, but there just isn't time. It is such a thrill to look down on the town and all the islands. Sometimes, though, all you can see is the mountaintops poking through the clouds."

"I know the thrill," Clara responded. "I climbed 12,000-foot Mt. Adams in southern Washington near my home when I was sixteen and am a member of the Mazama Club. You can only belong to that group if you've climbed a mountain with a glacier on it."

"Wow! You're lucky to have lived close to mountains all your life! Massachusetts only has little hills compared to these grand peaks in the West."

They had walked on to the New England Fish Company, and Emery showed her his office, and then they dropped in on Emma and Florence at home. August was still sleeping after his midnight shift.

On the way back through town, Emery bashfully pointed out Creek Street, which he said was probably the most active red-light district in the territory. "It's said to be the only place where both fish and fishermen go upstream to spawn," he said, sheepishly.

He told her he often wrote a check for a fisherman for several hundred dollars for their catch that NEFCO bought, only to have it to be blown the next night on Creek Street. Emery said there was hope, though, that the illegal businesses would be closed, because a citizens' group had met the year before and vowed to clean up the whole town.

By the time they were sadly saying good-bye, they'd agreed to write each other often. They'd discovered they had many of the same values, and they both loved the outdoors.

Clara had told Emery she grew up in Washington State, a few miles north of the Columbia River in the logging village of Willard, named for her father, Emil Willard. She left home to attend high school in Vancouver, Washington, and supported herself by checking railroad cars in the railroad yard during World War I. Then she went off to Bellingham Normal School (now Western Washington University). There her best friends were Enid and Jettie Stryker from the Kenai Peninsula, Alaska.

After teaching school in her home county of Skamania, she was ready for more adventure. Adventuresome she was, having climbed not only 12,281-foot Mt. Adams but also 10,781-foot Mt. Baker and 14,411-foot Mt. Rainier. She had been the first female fire lookout in Washington State, during her college years beginning in 1918. She spotted fires from Little Huckleberry Mountain near her family home for more than one summer. Her post was a tiny cabin on stilts with no running water or electricity. Occasional visits by foresters with horses bearing water from a distant stream were most welcome, because then she didn't have to carry the water herself.

In 1925 the Stryker sisters led her to her next adventure, when they told her of the teacher opening in Seldovia, Alaska. Little did she realize when she left Seattle what an impact on her future her decision to accept the position would be.

Almost-daily letters were in the mail from Emery. His letters grew more and more amorous. It wasn't long before Emery, too, boarded a ship headed for Seldovia. There they made plans for her to stop over in Ketchikan for several days between steamships on her way Outside at the end of the school year.

On her stopover, Emery was able to arrange a trip to the spectacular New Eddystone Rock, a 237-foot basalt spire that rises out of Behm Canal east of Ketchikan. After a picnic lunch there, what better time for Emery to propose marriage and for her to accept? They agreed to a wedding date of October 15, 1926, at her family home in Willard. It is there on New Eddystone Rock, now a part of Misty Fjords National Monument, that their ashes were placed after more than fifty years of marriage.

* * * * *

My Story

"A stork carried me to Ketchikan" is my stock answer to the perennial get-acquainted question "What brought you to Alaska?"

Often a blank look on the questioner's face reminds me that not many are familiar with that sex education phrase of eighty years ago. Parents used that stork story to answer questions about where their children came from.

Like my two Tobin family generations before me, Alaska has been a magical home. The sculptured mountains, mystical forests, generous ocean waters, tumbling rivers, and solemn lakes, besides the friendly people are, to me, essential elements to a happy adventuresome life.

Ketchikan was home my first twenty-two years. In-fluenced by my parents' (Emery and Clara) enthusiasm for the territory, I thought the twelve-foot yearly average rainfall felt invigorating and the storms exciting. Clear sunny days wiped out any negative remembrance of the rain being at all dismal during 24/7 downpours.

If it was raining, as it was on most days, we just wore appropriate clothing but didn't bother much with umbrellas, because we knew from experience that our clothes dried just fine. If the day was sunny, everything remotely resembling work was ignored in favor of get-ting out in one's boat for sightseeing, fishing, picnicking, camping, or for another hike up Deer Mountain.

Long before *Cheers* of TV fame, Ketchikan was a place where "everyone knows your name" and greeted you as you passed on the street. Smiles came from all who adapted quickly to the friendly atmosphere: Tlingits, the sweet odor of smoked fish sometimes emitting from them; suited bankers; girls wearing too much makeup from "the line"; unsteady clients of the many bars; Fili-pino cannery workers speaking in a language unknown to most of us; slicker-clad fishermen, the odor of fish follow-ing; and even the tourists carrying their umbrellas.

The earliest home that I remember was six and a half miles out South Tongass Highway where my folks staked a homestead. Dad built a house beside a rush-ing stream. Before Environmental Impact Statements were required, he dammed the flow for running water for indoor plumbing and for energy to run a generator to provide our electricity. Phone lines had already been strung from town. Later, it was interesting to me that my

Midwest college peers had grown up without running water, phone, or electricity while I had never been without them in the Last Frontier.

Being an only child, I was happy to play alone in the woods across the creek. Getting there was tricky, because I had to walk across a fallen slippery log. I was so scared of falling into the fast-flowing water that I stepped gingerly along the slippery surface, and it took me a long time to get to the other side. Once across, I built moss sanctuaries or picked blueberries that I could sell to the Alaska Steamship Company for a dollar a gallon. Blueberry pies were tourists' delight on their menu.

If there was a very low tide on a day I was home, I went across the road to the bedrock shore to explore the tide pools, where I was delighted to find purple and maroon starfish, hermit crabs in borrowed curly, spiral shells, an occasional needle-adorned sea urchin looking like a pin cushion, and darting minnows.

Mom was an avid gardener and soon had abundant vegetables growing in a little area where the dirt was deep enough. My responsibility was to gather gunny sacks full of seaweed and starfish to fertilize it. When it was harvest time, I learned how to dig out the potatoes. Oh, what a thrill it was to pull a big one out! I wondered how my joy compared to Grandpa's when he panned a large nugget.

* * * * *

Because of depression cutbacks, Emery lost his job at NEFCO but quickly was hired by the local newspaper. Shortly after he was hired, a group of local sportsmen, interested in sharing their enthusiasm for the abundance

THE FLIP OF A COIN

of fishing and hunting adventures, established a monthly magazine, *The Alaska Sportsman*. It was printed at the *Chronicle* where Emery worked. After only a few issues, the Sportsmen's Association could no longer keep it afloat.

Emery and a few other enthusiasts couldn't let it die. They thought there should be a magazine "Holding a mirror up to life on the Last Frontier." The first editorial said they viewed continuing the publication as their mission to tell "some of the adventures of the out-of-doorsmen in this great northern territory; of picturing its scenic grandeur, its romance, its fauna and flora."

Financing the dream continued to be a challenge for the twenty-three years the family published the magazine. When Mom sold Washington timber, the profit went into the magazine. They began and successfully ran a wholesale and retail souvenir business in order to support the magazine. They found investors who shared their dream. After selling our Mountain Point home to obtain some cash, we lived in a two-room apartment beside the print shop-bindery to save money. My folks' bed converted to a davenport by day. Single women rented rooms upstairs, which helped the cash flow.

After 1935 Mom and Dad were working sixty- to eighty-hour weeks starting up the magazine, so I stayed with my grandparents after school until my folks finished work, which was often near midnight. When I was in grade school, I waited down by the road for them to pick me up. Aunt Florence would walk me to the pick-up spot and stay until my folks arrived. If it was a clear night, Aunt Florence pointed out the different

119

constellations. Since there were few clear nights, I learned to recognize only a few of them.

After work Aunt Florence often took me down to the NEFCO dock to angle for dogfish, cod, or rockfish. Since the sewers dumped nearby, polluting the water, we never took the fish home to cook.

We became acquainted with a Greek cook who lived on one of the docked pile drivers. Aunt Florence took this opportunity to teach me the Greek alphabet so I could impress him.

Aunt Florence was a surrogate mother to me since she was single and could take time to play and teach me such things as the different breeds of dogs from flash cards she made with sample pictures of them. Flash cards of the fine arts enabled me to recognize famous paintings. Since she was gone all day working for the U.S. Lighthouse Service (later taken over by the U.S. Coast Guard), I had ample opportunity to play dress-up with all her clothes. Grandma allowed it, but Florence sometimes rebelled when she found her clothes scattered all over her bedroom. When I made her angry, I felt so guilty.

Other "toys" were ivory carvings Florence got by trading yard goods with St. Lawrence Island Eskimos. She had done some secretarial work for the well-known pseudo anthropologist, Otto Geist, who put her in touch with Natives he knew. I loved the tiny polar bears, various birds, kayaks, and cribbage boards all made from walrus ivory. Once she even received a sea mammal-intestine child's rain garment in exchange for some calico cloth. Since it had a distinct odor, she, not knowing its cultural value, got rid of it.

It wasn't often that we ate our dinner at home because my folks worked through the evening, but when we did, I particularly enjoyed the vegetables that came from our garden. When I went to the magazine office instead of Grandma's, we ate in restaurants. The adult portions I consumed probably contributed to my weight problem of today.

Mom and Dad were quick to take on almost every business opportunity they heard about, so when mink farming became lucrative in the 1930s, they built a mink house to accommodate about fifty mink. Since my folks were very busy with the magazine, they hired a man to come and feed the animals the canneries' leftover fish products. I didn't much like the screeching little animals and stayed away from them. I was warned that if I stuck my finger through the chicken-wire cages it might be bitten before I could pull it out. It wasn't long before the price of pelts took a nose dive, and we got out of the mink-farming business. Mom didn't even get a mink coat out of our efforts.

Home in the country was heaven to me my first eight years. When my folks decided, for economic reasons, to move from our country house to the building they'd leased for the business in town, I was so upset that I screamed and yelled that *I was not going to move.* I remember my father being so disgusted, that he threw something at me. He missed, and I thought that it was very funny. Of course, that fueled his anger, and he stormed out of the house. It was the only time I recall that he even raised his voice to me. I'm sure, now, that he was under a lot of pressure obtaining money to keep the magazine afloat and having to sell our house to do it.

The three of us often went on trips alone to the spectacular coves where fishing in nearby lakes was excellent. But Dad was so eager to have everyone enjoy the country that he chartered boats and invited friends, employees, and shop customers to join us for fishing or to see bear catching salmon at Naha Falls near Loring, about twenty-five miles north. We could count on seeing a hundred black bears a day at the peak of the pink salmon season.

Dad was particularly interested in having the U.S. Coast Guardsmen stationed at the local base join us and learn to enjoy the country. He may have been Ketchikan's first cruise director. Having gone with us on these trips, several homesick servicemen fell in love with the country and our employees and stayed to make their homes after the war.

Chapter 6

World War II Upsets It All

When I was twelve, I missed the fun of going to Naha Falls to see the bears. It was early in July 1942, and the Japanese had not only bombed Dutch Harbor but invaded the Alaska islands of Kiska and Attu. Mom and Dad thought I would be safe in Washington at Grandma Willard's, in case the Japanese were successful in occupying more of Alaska.

Everyone in Alaska was on edge after the surprise attack on Pearl Harbor and now an invasion of the Aleutian Islands. Not many Outside knew of the Japanese invasion of Alaska, because President Roosevelt put a blackout on news of the bombings and invasion. He thought it would make the citizens too upset to know that their homeland had been invaded.

Mom, Dad, and I stood on the Alaska Steamship Company dock watching the longshoremen secure the lines from the SS *Alaska* to cleats that would hold the ship secure. We hoped the men wouldn't slip on the wet deck as they pulled the lines with all their might. Mom and I were dressed in our Sunday best. She even wore her pretty grey hat with a veil. We were getting used to the idea that the two of us would be boarding soon for the two-and-a-half-day trip to Seattle.

Almost every year, Mom and I had gone south to visit Grandma Willard and the Loretts and DeWaters, Mom's sisters' families. Sherry Lorett and Barbara De-Water were my only cousins, and I looked forward to playing with them on their farms near Willard, where Mom grew up. This time I was even more eager for the journey, because I was going to stay with Grandma long after Mom returned home. I was eager to be on my own and learn how to do farm chores.

Dad helped us carry our luggage to our stateroom. The room was just wide enough for a single bunk bed and an aisle to the sink near the porthole, with its brass frame that could be locked tight by turning the screw lock to stop waves from splashing inside.

When all our luggage was stowed away, we returned to topside. A short blast of the whistle informed us it was time for Dad to go ashore. We went to the top of the gangplank to hug and kiss him good-bye. No sooner had Dad stepped onto the dock, the gangplank was hauled ashore, and the longshoremen unwound the lines from the cleats and threw them overboard to be hauled in by the ship's crew. While we threw kisses and waved until Dad was out of sight, the ship's massive engines came to life, throbbing like a heart as they turned the propellers to thrust us into the navigation lane.

I was eager to get back to our stateroom and crawl up onto the top bunk. I remembered the last time we went south; I had the top bunk and enjoyed watching the scenery through the porthole. On this trip, with the war going on, the round window had been blackened out. Even though I couldn't see out, I felt grown up sleeping on the top bunk. It wasn't very late and there was still sunlight, but I coaxed Mom into letting me get ready for bed. I was eager to climb to the top bunk. With the engines as a lullaby, I was soon asleep.

I was awakened in the morning by the music from a xylophone, which I knew from previous trips signaled that breakfast was being served. Fond memories of the elegant dining room coaxed me out of bed, ready to be served by the white-jacketed waiters when I decided from the printed menus what I wanted. Mom let me keep the menu because I liked the painting of the dog on the cover. The same artist, Josephine Crumrine, had painted a portrait of my cat, Puss. The picture had been a birthday present from my folks. By the time we reached Seattle, I had a whole collection of menus, each one with a different dog on the cover. I planned to give them to my cousins. The menus became popular collectors' items a short time later.

After breakfast we walked around and around the decks. Sometimes we stopped to watch porpoises play ahead of the bow. Games of shuffle board were usually in progress, and I was even allowed to compete in them, but I never won, even when I played against other kids my age who were also going "Outside for the duration."

We were lucky this trip not to encounter any very rough seas where the Inside Passage we followed was not protected from the open ocean by islands. I remember a previous trip that was so rough, I was seasick for more than a day when we went through the open water at Dixon Entrance.

From Seattle we sent Grandma a letter, telling her when we'd arrive on the train at Cook, the closest train stop to Willard. I was fascinated by the big city of Seattle. Unlike climbing to the top of Deer Mountain, riding the elevator to the observation deck on the thirty-fifth floor of the forty-two-story building of the Smith Tower was not exhausting, and the view of Seattle was just as awesome as looking down on Ketchikan from the ski cabin. Taking escalators in the Bon Marche was just as exciting as riding a Ferris wheel at Fourth of July celebrations at home.

Riding the train was pure excitement for me. I did get impatient, though, at how long the trip was taking, and I was glad to get to Centralia, the halfway point. In Vancouver, Washington, we boarded another train for the sixty miles east to Cook. Aunt Stella and Cousin Sherry were there waiting to drive us the last ten miles to Grandma's. Sherry, three years older than I, looked so grown up. I wondered if we'd enjoy playing house like we did the last time we were together.

Mom stayed with us a couple of weeks, then went back home, leaving me with Grandma Willard. What a great big change that was for me! She was a very hardworking woman, milking cows by hand very early in the morning and again in the evening. Mom and Dad had a very different schedule: working until almost midnight, then not getting up until noon.

Aunt Stella was in charge of the milk Grandma brought to the house to be bottled and delivered to customers in the village. Electric power was no longer available, because Stella's husband, who had installed the waterwheel-driven generator, had been killed by a falling tree three years before. No one else knew how to fix the mechanism. The house did have running water from Moss Creek. The frigid water, originating in the ice caves of Mt. Adams was used to keep food cool in a huge wooden box on the porch. Water ran into the box and reached about an inch in depth before draining. Food sitting in the water was kept as cool as if it were refrigerated.

After the cows had been let out and were well on their way to pasture, I went to the barn to play with kittens in the hay. Sometimes I stayed too long, and the cows came home to be milked. I was scared to death of these huge creatures that came right up to the door, preventing my escape. Their huge wet noses poked in the crack between the door and frame. I yelled and cried for someone to come and rescue me. Grandma dropped whatever work she was doing and came down to rescue me and give a thorough scolding about being scared of the placid cows.

I loved to go up the road to DeWater's to play with Cousin Barbara. She was only a year older than I and enjoyed making structures from fence posts as much as I did. On the warmest days, we could go swimming in the Little White Salmon River that ran through Big Cedars Park. When we walked to the park, we had to be very careful to get far enough to the edge of the road to let huge logging trucks pass safely with their loads of old-growth timber headed for the Willard mill.

When school started, I enrolled and attended with my cousins. I was in sixth grade, which was taught in the two-room school at Mill A, a short bus ride past Willard. By this time I was getting homesick. I missed my school pals at home. I wrote letters, begging Mom to come and get me. I circled in ink the tear drops that fell on the page as I wrote, telling about how no one cared much about me at school. Sherry didn't like to play outdoors, and Grandma didn't have time to help me when I was imprisoned in the barn by the cows. In a few weeks Mom came down to take me back home.

* * * * *

Ketchikan was still observing blackouts when I returned. Air raid wardens saw to it that not a light, not even a lit cigarette, was to be seen after dusk. In school we practiced what to do in case of an air raid, and we rather enjoyed the breaks in classes as we filed out into the woods or to hide in the cave of the Schoenbar Mine. Private boat owners were enlisted by the Coast Guard to help in reconnaissance. Fishermen reported sightings of submarines. Most of the perceived subs were just logs, but a few may have been actual sighting since certified encounters were made off the coast of Washington. When the ski cabin on Deer Mountain happened to burn down, the town folk were sure it was a signal for a Japanese invasion. They made sure we had a good evacuation plan.

Our Japanese residents, very respected businessmen and whose children were high achievers in school, were herded off to refugee camps in the western states. We remaining citizens thought it was a necessary procedure in this time of war and did nothing to stop these U. S. citizens' deportation. In Kotzebue, however, when concerned Native elders heard that their Japanese neighbors might be deported, they made a plan to hide their friends out on the tundra if ever a U. S. official stepped off a plane to round up their Japanese and German friends.

Residents from the Aleutian Islands were relocated to the abandoned Civilian Conservation Corps camp a few miles north of Ketchikan. Mom told me to have nothing to do with them because "they have lice." Considering the very poor sanitation conditions available to them, it was probably true through no fault of their own. Besides the camp being run down, it was situated among huge hemlock and cedar trees, an environment totally foreign to these people used to the wide-open spaces. Having been homesick myself, I had an idea of what their misery must have been like.

I had been spending all my spare time working in the bindery, helping to do everything to get *The Alaska Sportsman* ready to mail each month. I wondered when I was at Grandma's, *How is the bindery crew getting along without me?*

Assembling and mailing the monthly magazine was, at first, done above a dry goods store. It was there as a grade school student, whose parents let me think I could do just about anything, that I learned how to stamp out the subscribers' names and addresses on the addressograph, which used metal embossed plates. In fact, I was allowed to work at every aspect of the bindery production of the monthly magazine.

The magazine's earliest issues had the pages hand-creased with an ivory "bone." Collating the sheets with two pages on each side was first done by walking past the stacks of pages, picking up one from each stack as you walked by. Later, my dad invented a huge lazy Susan. By

129

this time a larger press printed four pages up. These were folded by a folding machine and stacked on the rotating table, where ladies sat and gathered the pages as they rotated by.

When the bindery moved to the new location, which included our apartment, we began printing the magazine there on our own press. I worked at composing the pages from the metal linotype "slugs" and photo "cuts" made of copper and wood. These cuts had to be ordered from Outside, a logistics nightmare during the war when shipping was irregular.

I was even allowed to run the linotype. Accuracy was not my strength, but it was fascinating to make the machine's arm come down, pick up my assembled line of type and deliver it to the molten pot of lead to mold each line of type.

When I was in high school, what made working in the print shop/bindery more interesting to me were the young men hired to run the Kelly press. One of these men was Gordon Bordine from Detroit, Michigan. He'd gone to Cass Technical High School and had learned printing, his passion. How exciting it was to flirt with and date a guy interested in printing and who had the use of his brother's Harley Davidson motorcycle! Donned in rain gear, on biking dates, we sped the thirty-six miles from one end of the road to the other. Oblivious to the pelting rain, we went on one adventuresome cycling date after another. Besides that, I believe we went to every movie shown in the two theaters. Theaters were more conducive to romance than rides in the rain on motorcycles. Riding motorcycles was not, however, my first choice of thrilling transportation.

Ever since fifth grade, when my desk was by the windows where I could watch the float planes take off and land in Tongass Narrows, I dreamed of learning to fly. As I watched the pontoons rise off the water, my heart rose with them. So beginning at age fourteen, I quit my summer print shop work and worked at the Sunny Point Salmon Cannery where the $1.04 hourly wage was higher than my folks could pay.

Cannery work was arduous, of course, but when working with others my age, it was always fun and sometimes not very serious at all. I worked with my best friend, arranging the fish that spilled out of a hopper onto a moving belt so that they were in order for the filler machine to cut them up and fill the cans.

I recall one time when the belt stopped, and we took off our canvas gloves to arrange our head scarves. All of a sudden the belt started up. We grabbed our gloves but I could only find one! My friend had hidden the other in one of the dozens of cleaned fish bellies. That fish went on to the filler, glove and all. We hoped some surprised cook was not too freaked out to find glove fingers in the can of salmon she was planning to serve for dinner.

That incident may have happened on one of the longer working days when we got giddy. We had to work until all the fish delivered from the fish traps had been canned, and some shifts lasted twenty hours but often were twelve or fourteen hours. We had happy thoughts about how much larger our paychecks would be rather than groan about the long work day.

After saving wages for three years for flying lessons, I soloed at age seventeen. What a rush it was at last taking off from Tongass Narrows on my own! On my required long cross-country flight, I'll never forget the looks of surprise on the faces of folks on the Bell Island dock when they saw the pilot of the plane that landed far out in the bay was a female, and a young girl at that. After I collected solo hours just eight hours shy of getting a private license, I decided I'd better save all the money I could for college and not continue expensive flying lessons.

There never had been a question that I would go to college. Nor did anyone guess my major wouldn't be journalism, so I searched for schools with the best journalism departments. The University of Minnesota was ranked about third in the nation for their journalism program. I saw that it was only one state away from Michigan. Close enough, I thought, to be able to continue my romance with Gordon, who had returned to Detroit after my high school graduation. His parents had come up to Ketchikan for a visit to see what their two boys had been doing. The four of them drove their car and motorcycle on a southern route home.

My college application was accepted at the University of Minnesota, and I made arrangements for my trip to Minneapolis. I'd take a plane to Seattle and a train on to Minneapolis. I wrote Gordon of my plans.

It seemed to be a very long trip alone. I was careful to not be vulnerable to any questionable persons. When I stepped off the train in Minneapolis, a well-suntanned man in a white shirt came up and asked if he could carry my bags.

"No thanks," I quickly replied. Then I did a double take. It was Gordon! I'd never seen him with a tan in rainy Ketchikan! He and his mother had driven from Detroit to welcome me to the Midwest.

I would have had a big problem finding housing had they not been there to help me. I had thought housing was assigned when you registered. We finally found a rooming house a few blocks from the campus.

My roommate, Marjorie Stronach, was a nurse with whom I still maintain contact. We roomed together all the years I was a University of Minnesota student.

I was used to being at the top of my high school class of twenty-nine students, so when I found myself making only average grades in classes that numbered four hundred students, it was very disturbing. I never thought of putting in any more study time than I had in high school. Even in journalism classes, I didn't excel. My top interest was in receiving almost-daily letters from Gordon. I could hardly wait for Thanksgiving and Christmas vacations, when I went to Detroit to be with him and his family.

I'd scarcely known what a "normal" family life was. Gordon's mother did not work outside the home. She, in my opinion, was then a perfect homemaker, and I dreamed of emulating her. I changed to a double major: journalism and home economics. Better grades in the home ec classes helped my self-esteem some, but the required chemistry and physics classes were my downfall. I'd had no background in those subjects.

By the time I was a junior, I was depressed about my average grades. Journalism wasn't as easy as I thought it would be, and my love life was too skimpy with Gordon at such a distance. I decided I could only find happiness by being with him. I quit college at the end of my junior year: 1951.

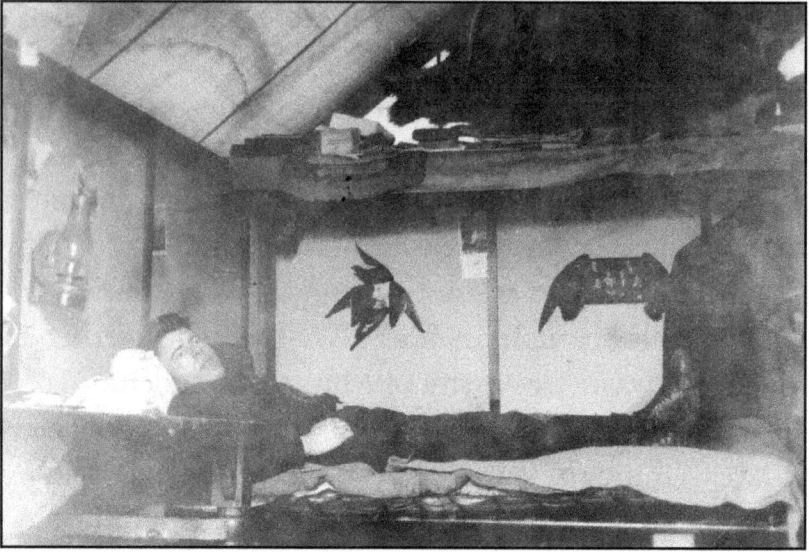

Emery Tobin daydreams in tent he and his father lived in 1920–1921, Ketchikan.

August Tobin, retired in Ketchikan ... twenty years of gold prospecting above the Arctic Circle.

Together at last in Ketchikan after twenty-four years separation: Emma, August and Florence Tobin.

Steps to solitude for August Tobin in Kamp Kliff, Ketchikan.

New Eddystone Rock where Emery Tobin proposed marriage to Clara Willard in 1925.

Tobin Home built by Emery at Mountain Point, six miles south of Ketchikan.

Clara Tobin bookkeeping for the magazine and souvenir business.

Grandma Emma Tobin babysat Doris Tobin while her parents worked long hours at The Alaska Sportsman.

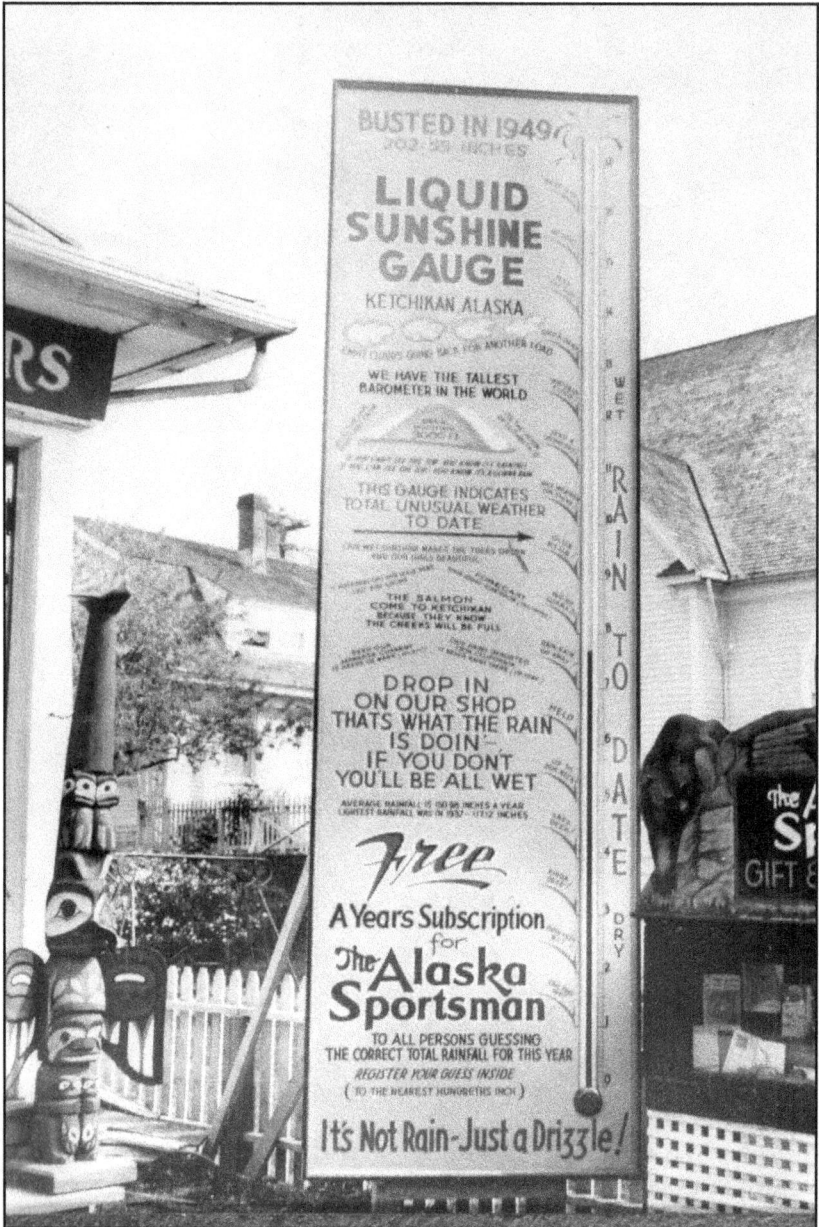

Rain gauge invented by Emery Tobin outside The Alaska Sportsman *office and Alaska Specialties souvenir store.*

Doris Tobin preparing for publishing business at age 6.

The Alaska Sportsman *employees on 1953 outing to Bell Island Hot Springs.*

Part Three

Chapter 7

Third Generation Makes Alaska Home

Gordon and I planned our wedding date for August 31, 1951, in Ketchikan. Two of my college housemates decided to attend. I had convinced them that they could earn next year's tuition plus the cost of their plane tickets by working in a salmon cannery or crab factory. This plan worked for them. In fact, one of them, Jan Olson, met her future husband, Don Ross, in Ketchikan that summer. She and her husband settled in my hometown. In 1963 she became Mrs. Alaska.

We were married in First Lutheran Church. My folks were not pleased, but they said little about how they felt. They didn't think quitting college after my junior year was a very smart thing to do. Besides, Gordon hadn't even been to college. He hadn't even finished high school!

Our first home was a lovely rental house right over the water of Tongass Narrows. High tides came up under the house. I worked for my folks, and Gordon worked in a small print shop. We were happy as the clams that lived only a few feet from our home. Soon we not only had a car but also a little inboard boat named the *Doris L.* We cruised around Revillagigedo Island to nearby inlets and coves every nice day we weren't working.

Our navigating skills needed honing, but we always made it back to port. Once, after tying up to the Thomas Basin Float, when we checked the bilge we were horrified to see the bilge water was almost reaching the floor boards. We'd hit a deadhead (partially submerged log) that punctured the hull. Instead of mooring at her berth, we motored out to our friend's with a dry dock where she could be repaired. We learned from that near disaster to always, always be on the lookout for anything in our way.

A favorite destination was Shoal Cove, a few miles south of Ketchikan in Carroll Inlet where there was a sand beach. We baited round crab pots, which were merely metal circles with chicken wire as a bottom. In a few hours we were hauling them up with enough Dungeness crabs for a feast on the beach. We could actually see the crabs venture onto the trap. We hauled them up quickly so they'd still be on the cylinder when it broke the surface. A campfire, some ten-gallon cans filled with salty sea water to cook the crabs in, and some mayonnaise for dipping the succulent crabmeat made a meal never to be forgotten. Some of the lowest tides occurred in the fall when storms were likely to blow in, curtailing our adventures.

It was not only winter storms that put an end to our carefree, outdoor activities, Gordon and I both had announcements that would change our habits drastically.

Just after the first of the year, I realized I was pregnant. We'd never even talked about having children, and I'm sure, if we'd planned on it, we wouldn't have chosen to be parents within a year of our marriage. I was not too enthused, but Gordon welcomed the news despite how a baby would complicate the dream he had.

When Gordon came home from a First Lutheran Church Council meeting in January, he shared something even more surprising than my news. He said he felt a call to the ministry! How could this be? It was not surprising, in one sense, since church meant a great deal to Gordon. He'd been very active in his Detroit church's youth activities. When we first began dating, it was important to him that I attend church with him. He'd been elected to the church council soon after joining First Lutheran Church.

What complicated the situation, now, was his lack of a high school diploma. He said he wanted to attend Luther College, Decorah, Iowa, and then Luther Seminary, St. Paul, Minnesota. Without a high school diploma, that seemed impossible.

I was glad that he wanted to go to college, but becoming a pastor seemed like an impossible dream. And then it meant I would be a pastor's wife! That most certainly was not a dream but a *nightmare*. Before I met Gordon, I had rarely attended church. And when I did, it was the Christian Science Church, which was a far cry from Lutheran in doctrine. My foreseeable future was, as I saw it, centered in business. And with Alaska now just developing, I was certain that whatever I did, it would be done in Alaska.

Pastors' wives were perfect, I thought. They played the organ or piano. They were perfect housekeepers. They raised perfect children. They knew Bible verses by heart. I had none of those attributes. I had never gone to Sunday School, where I might have become familiar with commonly used Bible verses. My family's housekeeping consisted of hurriedly cleaning up before expected company was to arrive. My chores were centered in the magazine publishing. I had never even had a babysitting job.

Iowa! How could I exist in Iowa where there were no mountains nor an ocean but just hot weather and corn fields? Nonetheless, at our wedding I'd heard the scripture, "Whither thou goest, I will go." I thought it was a vow all wives should make to their husbands. It took some time, but I decided that if God was calling, surely all would turn out OK. Later I learned that the scripture was a quote of Ruth to her mother-in-law!

I wondered, too, how we would manage a trip to Germany for the 1960 Passion Play in Oberamagau. We had talked seriously of this trip being a highlight for us. The play was presented only every ten years, and before our marriage, it seemed to be a possible goal for us.

* * * * *

My pregnancy was an easy one, and I was able to conceal it for several months, so I kept on working at the family business. Perhaps I, like Mom, didn't want folks (especially *my* folks) to "know what we'd been doing."

We agreed that we'd try going to Iowa and college "one year at a time." We made plans for our future in Ketchikan, if college and seminary didn't work out. We leased a ten-acre lot from the U.S. Forest Service on which to build a cabin. The annual lease fee was only ten dollars.

As soon as the weather allowed, we began building a cabin on the lot beside the Second Waterfall, two miles past the end of the North Tongass Highway, eighteen miles from Ketchikan. We had the lumber delivered to the dock at Knutson Cove, where we picked it up with the *Doris L* to transport to the lot. Sometimes we were so overloaded that if we'd gone through the wake of a passing boat, we would have swamped.

We stacked the lumber above the high-tide line. When we returned the following weekend every stick of lumber was gone! Had it been stolen? No, we learned that a storm had pushed the high tide higher than normal on the beach and floated the wood off and down Clover Pass. Someone told us they had seen two by fours drifting in the current. We had to replace the building materials using five hundred dollars we'd expected to cover our year at Luther. We barely had enough now to live on during the next nine months.

Gordon's brother had flown his own plane up from Detroit that summer, and he helped us with construction. Their mother, Alice, came late in July to help with the expected baby. In August when I continued building the cabin, Alice declared, "Gordon, some day you're going to make a very quick trip back in to town."

Finally, on August 26, Gordon's twenty-fifth birthday, we made that hurried trip to the hospital, and Carol Laurie was born. A week later, Gordon left for Iowa in our tightly packed 1952 Chevrolet Suburban.

The Ketchikan Superintendent of Schools, also a church council member, had cleared the way for Gordon to receive credit for his work on the Army's *Stars and Stripes* newspaper during the occupation of Germany after the war. Those credits completed requirements for a degree from Cass Technical High School, Detroit, and entry into Luther College.

Grandma Alice and I planned to fly to the Midwest as soon as we thought baby Carol could travel. She was three weeks old when we landed in Minneapolis, and Gordon was there again to greet me, but this time I was not alone, and the rendezvous was at the airport, not the train depot.

* * * * *

Alice continued on home to Detroit. The three of us drove to Decorah where Gordon had rented an apartment in the married-student housing: old army barracks scheduled shortly for demolition. Gordon had moved into this new home and already knew many of the neighbors. He chattered enthusiastically about his campus life as we drove south.

Although the deadline for applying for veteran's education benefits had passed, we were able to live on savings, his wages when he could work as a pressman for the Norwegian language newspaper the *Decorah Posten* (even though he didn't speak that language) and the two hundred dollars per month his folks sent. Gordon's dad, John, worked two jobs in order to be able to help us.

Our new home was very sparse, with only a table and chairs and a bed in each of the two bedrooms. In the front room an oil-burning stove was the heat source for the entire place.

We shopped garage sales for furniture, and in a few weeks John and Alice brought extra family furniture from

Detroit. We gradually got acquainted with our neighboring married students who also had small children. Next door was a family of five whose mother, Anvy, was a nurse. Oh, how I depended on her for advice and help! When Carol cried, I hurried to Anvy's door to ask what to do to make her stop. Or I referred to Dr. Benjamin Spock's book, *Baby and Child Care*. It was falling apart from use in a few months.

Studying was tough for Gordon, but unlike in high school, he was strongly motivated. I longed for home, where I daily had been inspired by the majestic mountains. Although the nearby Mississippi River landscape was interesting, it just didn't inspire me like tall mountains. Yet, I felt warmly welcomed and comfortable as I got to know the solid Midwesterners who were strongly tied to tradition.

Tradition was a new concept to me coming from The Last Frontier, where tradition hadn't had time to develop. I've always professed to like change. I think it's invigorating. Learning traditional habits made me feel at ease, on one hand, because I knew what to expect since "it's always been done this way." Yet, I was frustrated when my new ideas didn't go over very well. "Sonia always leads the Bible study" was the reply to my suggestion to take turns being leader.

Gordon passed all his classes the first year. That meant a second year was in our future at Luther. We planned to return to Ketchikan for the summer, because Gordon could make more money there than in Iowa.

We took out the back seat of the Suburban and set up a play pen for Carol. Thankfully, this was legal, because seat belt laws weren't on the books yet. I was thrilled to see new country as we sped west toward home. This was my first long trip by car. When we reached the mountains, I insisted on stopping each time a new peak came into view so I could take a picture. It was like seeing old friends.

The drive to Prince Rupert, B.C., took us a week. We chose to board a ship there instead of Seattle, because it cut both time and ticket money off the trip.

In Ketchikan, we moved in with Mom and Dad. It was as comfortable as slipping into a down-filled mummy sleeping bag on a camping trip, to again be enveloped in the printing activities. Gordon worked as a pressman for my folks full time and for another print shop as well. We cruised out to our cabin as often as possible. Our savings for the next year of college grew to an impressive total. Too soon the summer was over, and we headed back to college life again. Would this be our last year or only the second of eight that would prepare us for the ministry?

We thought of only one year at a time, but with the resolve of a sockeye salmon to return to its birth place, we looked forward to going back to Alaska with Gordon as the pastor of a church there.

Carol proved to be a good traveler in her playpen. Had she inherited some of Aunt Florence's love for traveling? Aunt Florence had retired and begun her new life of wandering, which eventually took her around the world three times. She visited us many times during those school years, always encouraging us with love and financial help.

Aunt Florence applauded our goal of travel to Europe to attend the 1960 presentation of the Passion Play in Germany, but we all knew it was unattainable that year. We thought we could to go to the next one in 1970.

Living in the married-student housing complex, we made friends with many couples in much the same situation as we: living on a frayed-shoestring income while preparing for professions, though we all had small children. We enjoyed visiting each other and babysitting for one another. Child-rearing techniques were generously shared as were budgeting tips. Dr. Spock was an authority who settled many disagreements about discipline. Almost every Friday we were enjoying a potluck at someone's home where lively discussions went on about whether to spank or not to spank.

We became close friends with the Cherwiens and the Ryes, who each had a child about the age of our Carol. Walt Cherwien was finishing his senior year with a music education major. "Rocky" Rye had an athletic scholarship to play basketball as he studied sociology. Marian Cherwien's father was a pastor, and Miry Rye's father had been a missionary in Madagascar. I was a "new Lutheran," having just joined the church when I was a student at the University of Minnesota. Despite our differences in church heritage, I loved to be with them and their babies. I thought I could learn from both women what it was like to be a pastor's family. After all, the moms were p.k.'s (pastors' kids).

In the fall, I began to wonder if it could be true. Was another baby on the way? Yes, it became clear we were to be parents again. After several months, I confided in Marian and Miry. What a surprise it was to learn that each of them was also pregnant. *It must be the water*, we mused when we learned of several other student-housing couples who were expecting.

"Yeah, it must be the water," Rocky declared. "Remember Sonia and John Knutson who left Luther last year? Well, they've been trying to get pregnant and haven't had any success. Last summer Mary and Art Larson took them a jar of water from here and guess what? They're due in March!"

Norman Keith Bordine was born May 6, 1954. He was quite young to travel, but being a very mellow baby, we started the long drive back to Alaska as soon as school was over,. Our summer was pretty much a repeat of the previous summer.

My Dad, however, was entrenched in his goal of ridding Ketchikan of the worst red-light district in the state. It had been thirty years since Emery had told Clara, on her original visit to the city, that the citizens had vowed to rid the town of this social blight. Nothing had been done, so Dad made it his calling to clean up the town.

We were happy to leave for college and not become involved in the investigation of illegal activities connected with the red-light district of Creek Street.

* * * * *

Ketchikan historian Louise Brink Harrington has written about Dad's investigation in *The Tenacious Emery Tobin*, excerpts printed here by permission. She attributed Emery's obsession to clean up the town to his dismay over his father's drinking problem.

> August Tobin was an alcoholic. Twenty years
> in the Arctic had taken their toll and he'd

dealt with his loneliness and lack of success by drowning it in a bottle. The problem haunted the family and they tried to cover it up as best they could.

Grandpa's alcoholism was a very well-kept secret, indeed. It was only a few years ago, before Ms. Harrington wrote about it, that a lifelong friend of mine told me that August was an alcoholic. Then it dawned on me that his irregular gait, that I'd witnessed when I was about five years old, was due to his being drunk. Then there was that mysterious barrel of stinky stuff I discovered behind the hen house. I remember that when I was about four years old, I asked Grandma about it. Her nervous behavior and her admonishing me never to go back there again had left me still wondering what it was. *Could it have been a barrel of beer? Possibly so.*

For years Tobin had trouble dealing with his father's drinking. He grew to hate alcohol and everything that went with it: saloons, bars, gambling, bootlegging, not to mention graft, prostitution and murder.

All these evils proliferated in Ketchikan and Tobin crusaded against them. He became most concerned about the growing number of mysterious deaths that smacked of murder but were never solved.

Every year a number of bodies floated down Ketchikan Creek in front of Creek Street and ended up in Thomas Basin. 'They pulled out about eight bodies of fishermen a year,' Tobin wrote in a letter to his daughter. 'They would get drunk and doped up on Creek Street.'

When not enough was done by the police department, Tobin began his own 'citizen investigation.' By working with certain 'honest policemen,' he learned of shocking crimes in the department itself: cover-ups, kickbacks, policemen who drank on the job, stole money from prisoners, and consorted with prostitutes.

He also investigated the office of the U.S. District Attorney. 'I found that serious cases were being disposed of by district attorneys in unusual and suspicious manners,' he wrote. 'In many cases no charge was filed even though the evidence showed that violence had occurred.'

During the early 1950s Tobin wrote articles, editorials, and letters-to-the-editor, informing the public of his findings. He wrote about a study done by the American Social Hygiene Association: When it came to prostitution, crime and corruption, Ketchikan was worse than 95 percent of all U.S. cities!

In 1953 he testified before a federal grand jury, revealing everything he knew about corruption. The grand jury indicted the police chief on four counts, which were reduced to 'conspiracy to permit prostitution.' The chief pled guilty and left town. The police captain pleaded guilty to the same crime, and was suspended, and the district attorney resigned.

'In the last one-and-a-half years there has been only one drowning in Thomas Basin,' Tobin exalted to a friend.

Back at school in Decorah, we read of Dad's efforts in his daily letters. We learned that many in Ketchikan thought the "line" was good for business. The "girls" were big spenders in the local shops. Creek Street was what made fishermen choose Ketchikan as the port where they could sell their fish, purchase gear for the next trip, and buy "entertainment" after a long time at sea. Emery's life was in danger from those who benefited from the status quo. Hoping to scare off those who threatened him, he bought a gun to display on his desk.

Both Gordon and I were busy with school assignments. I'd decided to take physics and chemistry classes in order to earn those credits in classes I'd failed at the University of Minnesota. This time around I aced the subjects.

When spring came and it was time to plan a return to Ketchikan so Gordon could earn money for his last year of college, we thought it was best that I stay in Decorah because I was pregnant! We figured I was due the last of July. Wrong!

This time, Gordon flew back to Ketchikan where he worked two full-time jobs. Almost-daily letters from him said "it was still raining." It was a near-record rainfall that year, approaching the 1949 record of 202.55 inches or over sixteen feet.

Oh, how I envied him in that cool invigorating rain! It was my first summer out of Alaska since I spent time at Grandma's in Washington State. The temperature at the student housing was 110 degrees for ten days. *Why would anyone ever live here permanently?* I wondered.

July came and went. Obviously we'd miscalculated my due date. My days consisted of getting Carol and Norman ready for the wading pool where the three of us would spend the day. It was about all I could do to waddle across the road to that oasis of relative endurable temperature. I sat with my feet in the shallow pool, hoping for relief while kids waded and often splashed me. Finally, on August 22, I called my good neighbor Anvy and told her I was ready to go to the hospital. She drove me there and stayed with me until about twenty-two hours later, Janet Lynn was born. Oh, she was so cute with chubby cheeks and pointed chin. It was worth going through a breech birth to receive her. Gordon arrived a couple of days later and brought us home from the hospital.

In three years our family had grown from two to five members. I was ready to give up on the rhythm method of birth control. *How can we afford college for three? Will there be more babies? We really can't afford a doctor's appointment. Yet, we can't afford not to use some other birth control method that would work. But in Iowa, is it still illegal to give out birth control information?*

Without telling any of our friends, I made a doctor's appointment. There were such strong feelings against birth control that I was scared of what people would think of

156

me. After all, it had been less than two dozen years since the 1873 federal Comstock Law had been repealed. That law had made it unlawful to disseminate "immoral articles," which in reality meant "birth control information."

Gordon drove me to the doctor's office I'd visited a few times before Janet was born. In the waiting room I wondered what my doctor would think about my request. It was still believed by many that preventing conception was against God's wishes and against the law. Had the nurse not called me after about an hour's wait, I think I might have left. It was only a short time before my doctor and his nurse came into the examining room and I had no chance to escape.

He asked me why I wanted to use birth control. I explained to him we'd had three kids in three years and that we couldn't afford to have more. The rhythm method just wasn't working for us. I recall clearly how the doctor excused the attending nurse from the examining room. There would be no witness to what he was going to tell me and prescribe. He proceeded to give me the valuable, legal, but religiously unacceptable information and prescription for the diaphragm I wanted.

We had grown very close to the Cherwiens and Ryes. Walter Cherwien had graduated and was teaching in a nearby town. When the three families lived in the student housing, we began a tradition of having Thanksgiving dinners together. This tradition I liked! We continued this over the years until the Cherwiens and we enjoyed twenty-three turkey days together. Tradition had become important to me. The Ryes had moved to California and we had lost track of them.

One thing that bound us together was that each time we added a baby to our family, the Cherwiens and Ryes did the same. We had much in common raising our families. We babysat each others' kids. We shared budgeting tips. Kids' clothing was passed around. The fathers carpooled to school. Together we cheered Luther's basketball and wrestling teams to wins. We exchanged our best recipes for inexpensive dishes and went on sightseeing trips around the state.

The Indian Mounds, burial grounds, were highly recommended as places of interest. Mounds! I was lonely for mountains! Yet, it was a lovely park and we mused with our extended family about the original inhabitants' lives. It was natural for me to accept others as "family" since my folks, like most Alaskans, had few family members in the territory and they "adopted" friends they particularly enjoyed as family. An extended family was what I was used to. Our guests at gatherings didn't need to be blood relatives to be included and enjoyed.

Now Gordon had only one more year of college before going on to Luther Seminary in St. Paul. *We'll be back in Alaska in just five more years!* We had moved to Iowa with only the packed Chevrolet Suburban. Moving to the Twin Cities required a trailer as well as our van.

As we traveled north to Minneapolis, I wondered if by some miracle we could travel to Germany to the Passion Play in Oberamagau for its 1960 presentation. Perhaps there was a scholarship the seminary offered for study abroad. Aunt Florence was keeping my desire to travel overseas alive with her adventure stories from India.

158

* * * * *

Gordon's home church in Detroit began to subsidize our seminary expenses. We were eligible for low-income housing in "The Project" in Minneapolis, where several other seminary students lived. Gordon got a part-time job with a printing company. Seminarians living in the Project carpooled to school in St. Paul.

Again, we shared cost-cutting practices with seminary friends. We bought sides of beef to split between families and to store in our frozen-food lockers. Whoever went to the bakery, shopped for day-old bread for several families. The farmers' market provided our fresh produce. We reconstituted powdered milk by shaking it in the new Tupperware that was so popular. We made virtually all meals from scratch. The kids learned to paste into booklets the redeemable S & H green stamps, given out with grocery purchases. Household items such as silverware, knives, and dishes could be obtained by turning in filled booklets. The kids, though, no longer had the chore of coloring margarine by puncturing the orange-colored dot and then massaging the margarine, encased in a plastic bag, until the color resembled butter. Iowa, being a dairy state, had made it illegal to sell colored margarine. In Minnesota colored margarine was available for purchase, at a much lower price than butter.

Chapter 8

Midwest Parish Life

After his first year at seminary Gordon got a position as interim pastor for the summer at Saco, a three-point parish in eastern Montana. That meant that he preached in three different churches each Sunday. The most distant one was an hour's drive from our parsonage. This was big scale grain-farming country. What strong personalities we got to know there! *How can they be so optimistic*, I wondered, *when they often experience tornadoes or heavy rainstorms that wipe out their ready-to-harvest crops of grain? I guess they, like Alaska fishermen, know Mother Nature is in charge of their success or lack of it. Alaska fishermen have to rely on good weather to harvest their "crops" of salmon too.*

One hot Sunday afternoon, as we drove out toward the Nelson Reservation and Recreation area, I was visualizing home and began to compare the scenery around us with what was familiar in Alaska. *You know, this country could grow on you. I love to see the expanse of wheat fields but, on the other hand, I sure miss the mountains. It's kinda nice to be able to plan an outing like this and know it's not going to rain. Here they go to such great lengths to catch and save each drop of water. Those irrigation ditches sure make it easy for this country to win any mosquito population density contest. Alaska's supposed to be famous for its big mosquitoes, but I think Montana takes the prize for quantity. At least at home we don't have to use our airplanes to spray towns to get rid of the pests. I think the cactus around here are really marvelous. They hang in there with only a few drops of water each season. If we should go without rain at home for a week, the plants look like they're ready to blow away.*

The reservoir areas were usually developed into recreational spots, where pronghorn antelopes thrived and migrant birds found a good stopping place. These wildlife refuges were new to me. I don't think we had any in Alaska. At home there was plenty of space for the animals to roam without anyone having to set aside "safe areas" for them. Seeing majestic antelope proudly roaming happily in these places where they were protected was, for me, a special gift. The land was devoid of trees, but I appreciated the golden fields of wheat, waving constantly in the wind, for their beauty.

Not being limited to the thirty-six miles of road in Ketchikan was exciting to me. We could actually drive to Saco Hot Springs. If we wanted to bathe in the healing waters of Bell Island Hot Springs, about fifty miles north of Ketchikan, we had to go by boat or plane. We drove to such places of note within several hundred miles of Saco. The refuges and reservoirs were like magnets attracting us, because we all could enjoy swimming and bird and animal watching there.

After his second year at seminary, Gordon was again given a summer interim assignment. This time he was to serve in western Wisconsin near Colfax, which had just experienced a devastating tornado that flattened the town. Knowing that we would be in tornado country worried me. News of such storms sent chills up my spine.

The parishioners in this area were also farmers. When Gordon saw that some of the worshippers were dozing off during his sermons, he felt his sermons must be very boring.

"I try so hard to come up with a meaningful message each Sunday, but I don't think my lessons get across. They just don't seem interested, and several of them are sleeping before I've said a dozen words," he complained.

"Well, just remember, hon, they've already been up and done a day's work before coming to church. At least they're here. I'll bet you'd be catching a few zzz's if you were in their place even if it were God himself speaking."

"I guess you're right. I'll just have to do the best I can."

* * * * *

The third year of seminary was usually spent as an intern at a church. Since Gordon had been filling in as pastor during summers, the year-long intern requirement was waived and he was in his last year at seminary. With a sockeye salmon's determination to return home, we believed we'd be called back to my home and to a parish back in Alaska when Gordon finished seminary. That hope was how I endured being away from my home territory for seven years.

I longed for friends who were often thinking of new ways things could be done; who had endured the often tough conditions the frontier offered; who loved the outdoor activities of mountain climbing, fishing, hiking, boating, and camping. I was also longing to take that trip we'd planned to the Passion Play in Oberammergau, Germany. Before our wedding, we had planned the trip for 1960. It was now 1959. Apart from some unforeseen miracle, the trip was financially out of reach for this presentation. Aunt Florence's world travel stories were still firing my longing for a trip to Europe.

Imagine our surprise when the only call Gordon received at the end of seminary was from a church in northern Minnesota! The town of Remer was about a three-hour drive north of Minneapolis. The main industry had been logging, but now many of the men drove to the north shore of Lake Superior to work in the taconite industry. There was, however, still one lumber mill in town. The population was about five hundred, a large percentage of whom belonged to Bethany Lutheran Church. Businesses included one of almost every kind that one would need to live a simple life in the community. There was a Red Owl grocery store, a drug store, bank, gas station, and three other churches. Huge pine trees, like sentries guarding the wilderness, still remained around the periphery of the town. Folks from the Twin Cities came to vacation here: camping, ice fishing, or sightseeing.

It was a two-point parish which means that the pastor was in charge of two churches. The other church was Our Savior Lutheran in Outing, an unincorporated town, a twenty-minute drive south. Each Sunday after conducting services at Bethany, Gordon drove to Our Savior Lutheran to do the same. The parishioners there had recently built an A-frame church building.

Outing, situated on the edge of a lake, was the center of popular tourist vacation spots in Cass County near well-known Brainerd. Unlike many churches whose attendance goes down during the summer, Our Savior's attendance multiplied when vacationers and folks who owned cabins nearby came to worship. The new church building was large enough for many events like potluck meals, Sunday school, and rummage sales.

The Bethany Church building in Remer, just kitty corner from the parsonage, had served the community for scores of years, yet it offered only worship space. There was no running water, no room for social activities, nor Sunday school classes. The church office was in the parsonage.

The parsonage had been well maintained throughout its decades of use. There was a new enclosed porch with a door to the office, skirting entry into our living room. Four bedrooms upstairs lined the hall leading to the bathroom. I was determined to exemplify the "perfect pastor's wife" by being an excellent housekeeper, so I kept the living room spick and span with no child's toys visible. I soon realized, however, that everyone who came to visit came to the back door leading into the kitchen, which was always a mess with flour from bread making still on the floor, the scraps of gift vegetables remaining in the sink, and dishes from the last meal scattered on the table. So much for my trying to role-play the perfect pastor's wife!

Since the school was just down the street Carol, in second grade, and Norman, a kindergartner, walked the short distance to classes. Because the town was near an

Indian reservation, many Chippewas went to school in Remer. It seemed to me that half of the first grade class came from that population. I was surprised to learn none had ever graduated from Remer High School. The Natives here were not experiencing as comfortable a lifestyle as the Natives I knew in Ketchikan.

We wondered if we would have any meaningful contact with these people from the Leech Lake Indian Reservation. None were in the habit of attending our church services. It wasn't very long before our question was answered. A Cass County social worker came to ask Gordon if he would be the guardian for Alice Burnett. This meant that he would receive her welfare checks and pay her bills at the local Red Owl grocery store. Alice was a victim of alcoholism and was not prompt in paying her debt. Her several children had been placed in foster homes, where the county believed they would have a better life.

Gordon agreed to the assignment and got acquainted with Alice, a very quiet woman who came to the parsonage to talk, occasionally.

I was happy when she was willing to do ironing for me from time to time when alcohol was not in charge of her life. She ironed very carefully; each pleat creased perfectly. I wished she'd been around for hire when the girls were wearing their frilly dresses made in the Philippines, which were popular when the girls were toddlers. I was happy to be relieved of the ironing chore. Once, however, I noticed the wrinkles in a bed sheet (yes, we ironed sheets then) she was working on, weren't being smoothed out. I soon saw why. She'd forgotten to turn the iron on. We both laughed when I pointed it out to her.

Alice knew she could count on Gordon's help. One call from her came about two in the morning. Carol asked about it as we drove to a synod church meeting.

"Dad, I heard the phone ring in the middle of the night and then you left. Did someone die?"

"No, hon," Gordon replied. "It was Alice. She needed a ride home from a bar out past Walker. I was glad she called because she was almost unable to walk and needed to be home. I had to drive like this" he said as he jerked the steering wheel to the right. "She went to sleep and leaned over on my side. A sudden turn pushed her back on her side."

Just then, flashing lights signaled that the highway patrol was after us. The kids were petrified. When the patrolman came up to the car he leaned in very close to Gordon as he questioned him about his erratic driving. When he detected no alcohol on Gordon's breath, he let us go with a warning to drive sensibly.

We began thinking that we could enjoy having another child in our family, but increasing the family would strain the budget. We decided to apply for a foster child whose expenses would be paid by Cass County. Billy Mitchell, a Chippewa Indian, joined our family when we'd lived in Remer a couple of years. He was seven years old but in the first grade. He'd lived with four other foster families. He'd been frequently moved because he had developmental problems that families found hard to deal with. He'd originally been taken from his single, alcohol-addicted mother who didn't care for him adequately. She had passed away at the age of thirty-two.

Billy was a quiet, meek child who fit in well, although his habit of always being the last one to finish any task or finally come for meals and outings tested our patience. He had a very noticeable purple scar on his neck and face where a birth mark called a hemangioma had been removed surgically. I'm sure he felt quite unattractive. Repeating the first grade did little to help him catch up to grade-level expectations. It was frustrating for both of us when I worked with him on his school work. He tried very hard but he just couldn't retain what we covered. We'd never heard of fetal alcohol syndrome, which makes recall impossible.

Remer was an example of what Hillary Clinton meant when she said, "It takes a village to raise a child." We'd been advised to not make special friends with any particular parishioners but to be friends with everyone. That advice was hard to keep when we got to know the Browns who had four daughters about the same age as our kids. We soon were together often. I learned many homemaking skills by being with this family.

The government might classify most of Cass County residents below the financial poverty level, but what was lacking in financial wealth, was made up for in their fortunes of faith, endurance, creativity, and family values. I was soon copying their lifestyle by making our bread, gardening and canning the produce, sewing the children's clothes by sometimes using our cast-off adult garments for material. Many parishioners supplemented our income by supplying us with milk, and other foodstuffs they produced. Harold Myers dubbed himself "Dutch Uncle" to the kids and played the part of a benevolent family relative who entertained the kids and always paid attention to them.

We were happy to have Aunt Florence visit several times. One of her most memorable visits was when she returned from over a year in India. Her stories of establishing a prosthesis manufacturing venture in Kottayam, Kerala, India, stirred up dreams of our travel to places farther than Germany to see the Passion Play in 1970. She and a friend, Glen Marl, had worked together to teach workers how to make prostheses for the many victims of polio in the area. After over a year developing the business, they turned it over to the local residents to operate.

* * * * *

In the background of church life was a desire for a bigger, more useful church building. Gordon fed this yearning with messages, encouraging them to believe that a new church could be built. Harold Myers, embracing faith that a new church could be in the future, donated land for it. The council held many meetings, planning to make it happen. A professional fund-raiser was hired. He trained teams how to go out and contact neighbors who could buy, at a good interest rate, church bonds that would mature at different periods of time.

Finally everything was ready to present the bond opportunity to the public. The goal was twenty thousand dollars. Raising these funds was expected to be a huge project lasting several weeks. The dedicated members, armored with faith, covered the community in one night and reached the goal. Some bonds were bought with cash, literally pulled out from under mattresses.

An architect's plan was approved. Logging parties were formed, and trees were felled. Horses were located and enlisted to drag the logs out of the woods. The timber was exchanged at the sawmill for the lumber needed for building. It wasn't long before the members had poured the foundation and the building was underway. Women provided food and encouragement, and some worked as carpenters alongside their husbands.

When completed, the new church seemed immense. There were plenty of seats for everyone each Sunday. Worshippers could remain for coffee in the basement social hall as they waited for their children to finish Sunday school in other rooms. The pastor's study provided counseling and study space.

When we'd served this parish seven years, we received a call to Hope Lutheran Church in Moose Lake.

With a name like "Moose Lake," one might have thought we were at last headed back to Alaska, but this town was about a hundred miles east of Remer. We were impressed with the congregation's dedication to their church building. The building was a lovely brick structure with stained-glass windows and all the space and amenities one could want. The economy of the town was centered on the Moose Lake State Mental Hospital, where many in the community worked as professional caregivers.

Maybe with our increased income we could manage a trip in 1970 to the Passion Play. When Aunt Florence visited us in Moose Lake, she told about how she traveled on a limited budget. She'd now circled the globe three times, visiting sixty-three countries but was ready to settle down. She had chosen Woodburn, Oregon, as

169

her permanent home and invited us to visit as soon as we could.

The call presented a challenge to serve a large congregation. The people were largely of Scandinavian heritage. The church employed a parish worker who relieved Gordon of work he didn't feel qualified to do, like office chores and typing. She also directed youth activities.

We decided to accept the call. Taking Billy with us was complicated since he'd be going out of Cass County's jurisdiction; but the red tape was cut, and we were given permission to keep him with us.

When we'd been in Moose Lake a few months, a call to be the pastor at Our Savior's, Nome, Alaska, came. Oh, how tempting it was to consider accepting, but we didn't feel it was fair to the folks at Hope to leave them so soon after they'd moved us to their town. With some hesitation, Gordon returned the call with his regrets.

Our parsonage was in the center of Moose Lake whose population was about three times Remer's. It was beside the old abandoned church, which was soon to be torn down. The church council had already been talking about selling the parsonage. Its sale would give the church money to invest and give the pastor a housing allowance so he could have equity in property for retirement. The decision was made to go ahead with that plan, and we bought a house four miles from town on a lovely lake. There was some talk about the pastor not being accessible so far from the church building, but it soon died down.

Living on the lake was an almost perfect lifestyle for us. In the summer we enjoyed swimming and canoeing. In the winter we snowmobiled. We kept two snowmobiles in order to have one that was operational. Teenage kids are likely to cause various breakdowns in their aggressive use of the machines. Besides, we never could afford new machines that might have gone without repair for longer periods of time.

The 1970 presentations of the Passion Play were coming closer, but the added expenses of teenagers and catching up on living expenses left no monies for such a trip now, either.

When Carol's college expenses would soon be in our budget, I decided I should finish the degree I started at the main campus of the University of Minnesota by going back to school at the University of Minnesota Duluth. We were only forty miles south of the school. I lined up car-pooling rides with several Moose Lake students attending UMD and began work on a home economics education degree. Thankfully, all my credits from the main campus of the UM, plus those from Luther College were accepted.

This was a time when women were just beginning to work outside the home, and to have a pastor's wife adopt that lifestyle was quite unusual. It was a far cry from the picture I had originally had of a pastor's wife. The Home Economics Department head seemed a bit behind the times when she required me, like the single students, to live in the Home Management House for six weeks, where I could learn how to manage a home. This meant leaving my own family for that period. My family was agreeable to the inconvenience, and we concentrated on the learning they, too, would get from the experience. The department head was not convinced there were jobs for us married women when we graduated, so I was somewhat smug when I was the first in my class to secure a job when I graduated in 1969. It was at Moose Lake State Mental Hospital.

As the home economics teacher of mental patients who were about to be discharged, I taught homemaking skills they may have forgotten after many years of institutional living. My patients joined me in an apartment-like setting on the top floor of the hospital. I enjoyed working with these folks who seemed very happy to be in the classes of cooking, homemaking, nutrition, and sewing. I never had to call for assistance in managing an upset student. We went on field trips to shop for groceries and invited hospital staff to meals we prepared.

This was during a time when there were efforts to discharge as many patients as possible by treating them with medications. When I left, the hospital population of seven hundred had dwindled to about half.

Daughter Carol's high school graduation present from us was a set of luggage. We were eager to see our kids try out their wings. Probably because she'd heard so much about my hometown, she decided to spend the summer in Ketchikan, where she could stay with my cousin. She'd heard of all the work possibilities, so was not concerned about getting summer work that would add to her college savings. She got a job at the hospital as an aide. It did pay somewhat better than what employment in the Midwest might have produced, but the Alaska adventure was not what she had hoped. The Midwest lifestyle was what she looked for. She stuck it out for the summer and came home just in time for college.

When Carol went off to Concordia College, Moorhead, Minnesota, we had the opportunity to host, for a year, an American Field Service exchange student from Ethiopia. Tiegistu "Tig" Lemma was a brilliant eighteen-year-old who learned rapidly in high school and made friends with almost everyone he met. It wasn't long before he had a very good command of the English language. When he returned to Ethiopia after a year with us, he had received a coveted scholarship to Haile Selassie University, Addis Ababa, the only college in Ethiopia. Shortly after he got back to his home country, the university was closed because of unrest in the country. *What a waste of a mind.*

Son Norman thought that living up to a congregation's expectations for a p.k. (pastor's kid) of being a "perfect child" was a bit difficult. Everyone knew who he was, and he felt under scrutiny all the time. He thought getting into trouble like "normal teenagers" brought a stronger-than-usual negative evaluation from some church goers. Yet, we never admonished him to behave any better than anyone else. He worked at the local Peterson Drug Store most of his high school years. There he developed an interest in two subjects: pharmacy and the boss' beautiful blonde daughter, Tracey Peterson. When he graduated from high school in 1972, he went on to North Dakota State University to work toward a degree in pharmacy. He continued to pursue the affections of his high school classmate. Finally in his junior year, he and Tracey decided to marry. We were so happy to have Tracey join our family. Like his mother, he married at age twenty-one, but he didn't quit school like I did. We thought they made a lovely couple. Norman and Tracey began their married life in a mobile home near NDSU campus in 1975.

Billy struggled in high school, falling behind, yet being promoted to each successive grade. When one class was studying Indian history it was mentioned that "There are no Indians in Moose Lake."

"Oh, yes, there are," someone replied, "Billy Bordine *used* to be an Indian!" We had, as was the practice at that time, tried to assimilate Billy into our culture, completely ignoring his heritage. He felt out of place and began running away without any perceivable warning. Cass County would retrieve him. Once he hitchhiked as far as Oklahoma and was flown by commercial airline back home. That pleasant flying adventure only fueled his desire for more.

Finally, Billy was assigned to a group home in Duluth. From there he continued to flee. When they were preparing him to join the U.S. Coast Guard, he was just about to succeed, but he ran away again. It seemed hard for him to anticipate the experience of the unknown pattern of success. It was a habit he was to repeat in the coming years, and we lost track of him.

Carol's graduation from Concordia was quickly followed by her wedding on June 1, 1974, to John Weitzel. We were ever so glad to have John in our family. John had been in Carol's college class and was a quarterback on their football team. The couple moved to Ankeny, Iowa, where he worked for a freight company, and Carol got a job in personnel with a junior college.

Janet, too, received luggage as a high school graduation present and used it when she returned to Ketchikan.

She had spent the summer between her high school junior and senior year there. She enjoyed that experience more than her sister, and Janet returned after high school graduation.

Chapter 9

Back to Alaska

When we'd been at Hope for about eight years, we felt a growing antagonism against us. It was heartbreaking to experience rejection by the people we'd come to love and serve. Sometimes when I joined a group of women, I could immediately feel the social atmosphere turn as cold as if I'd entered Grandpa's New England Fish Company's cold storage workplace.

Gordon brought home reports that all the council members talked about at meetings was the financial situation of the church. Some personal offerings were dedicated to only the church-building mortgage, and none of the money was to go to the salary of the pastor. I heard of stories of Gordon's supposed infidelity. *Could hell be any worse? Were these rumors starting with the church secretary?* There was neither performance evaluation nor confrontation of any wrong doing.

Gordon, not having the support of the church council, finally resigned. Quitting without another call was professionally very serious. Several weeks later, while attending a meeting of bishops of several districts, Gordon received a call to Soldotna, Alaska. My first reaction was: *Soldotna? I've never heard of it. I don't remember addressing any of* The Alaska Sportsman *maga-zines to that town.*

Then I learned that Soldotna, a hundred forty-five miles south of Anchorage, was a relatively new town to the territory. The post office was established in 1949, af-ter land had been opened up on the Kenai Peninsula for homesteading. Now in 1975, it was a rapidly growing town of about twelve hundred, double its 1960 popula-tion. Gordon made a quick visit there to Christ Lutheran Church and decided to accept the call.

We sold our lake home and packed all our belong-ings into a two-and-a-half-ton moving truck that we'd pur-chased. One November day in 1975 we hitched our VW Bug to the back of the truck and took off, at last, for Alaska.

* * * * *

Driving the Alaska Highway in the dead of winter wasn't bad at all, because snow filled in the ruts and pot holes. The challenge was to have enough gas to take us, preferably when it was still daylight, to the next gas sta-tion that remained open in winter. The crossing of the Canadian border and into Alaska was not the euphoric event that we might have expected, because the officials handed us an unexpected bill for using their highway to transport our (personal) freight.

When we got to Glennallen, about three hours out of Anchorage, we called my Swedish cousin, Pastor Carl-Erik Mawe, to let him know about when we'd arrive at his Alaska Methodist University home. He and his wife, Margareta, held Swedish-language teaching positions there while Carl-Erik was researching material for his doctorial dissertation.

177

He was curious about "traditions" and had been traveling across the United States to interview descendents of immigrants from his hometown, Uppsala, Sweden. He would write his book on what, if any, Swedish traditions were practiced in their American homes. Did they still eat *lutefisk* (cod dried in lye)? *Lefse* (a burrito-like thin bread made from potatoes)? Did they still open Christmas gifts on Christmas Eve or Christmas Day? He actually was surprised to find that the immigrants were still eating lutefisk during their Christmas celebrations. The Scandinavians in the "old country" had given up that practice long ago in favor of more tasteful means of preserving fish.

The Mawes told us stories about Sweden, which added to Aunt Florence's enticing tales of Europe, and I wondered if we could perhaps fly over the North Pole in five years to realize our dream of going to the 1980 Passion Play in Germany and travel to Sweden. Flights out of Anchorage over the North Pole had considerably reduced ticket prices. Little did I know that twenty years would pass before I would see Sweden.

It was so good to see the Mawes again. They and their children had visited us in Moose Lake a few years before. Carl-Erik's bushy eyebrows looked identical to Dad's. Maybe he'd inherited his jovial personality from that side of the family too, for Carl-Erik was lots of fun.

As we caught up on what they'd been doing, I thought, *He's met every Swede in the whole State of Alaska!* He had interviewed immigrants out in the Aleutian Islands, thirteen hundred miles from Anchorage, where Swedes had taken up their profession of fishing brought over from "the old country."

The next morning, after a delightful traditional Swedish breakfast of *plattar* (small crepe-like pancakes) like the ones Grandma Emma used to make, we took off on the last leg of our trip. Driving around Turnagain Arm, I thought, *It's so beautiful! It feels like home with the mountains so close.*

As we drove on through the Kenai National Wildlife Reserve, I watched for moose in every marshy area. I was sure one was looking out at us. I smiled as we went through a burned-over area where the trees were stripped of their foliage except for a tuft at the top. *They DO look like they could be Alaska cattails, as described in* The Milepost!

When we reached Soldotna, we easily located the little ranch house parsonage, just a few blocks from Christ Lutheran Church. We had thought ahead, when packing the truck, and left the bedding in an accessible spot. A bed was the most important piece of furniture to us at that moment, so we quickly set it up and soon were asleep. As we dozed off, we hoped we'd not have nightmares about unpacking the rest of the truck.

The next day many friendly, welcoming church members came to help us with unpacking. There was no need to worry about how to get everything unloaded. We felt like we'd known these new friends for years. I evaluated the three-bedroom, one-bathroom house and decided it would be a very cozy and efficient home for us.

We scheduled an open house for the community and had the invitation put in the local paper. Shortly before anyone arrived for the open house, I got a phone call. "Do you remember Alice Burnett? She's my mom, and she's visiting me here in Kenai, just twenty miles away. Can we come to your open house?"

"Of course!" We were thrilled to have these former Remer folks with us. Alice had "gotten saved" and was now a recovering alcoholic of many months. In Remer there were times when she had trouble walking across the street. How could she travel four thousand miles to Alaska?

Alice's daughter had met her husband at a Southwest school for Natives. He was from a Yup'ik village on the northwest Alaska coast. Alice was having the time of her life visiting her children around the States.

Alice looked great. She beamed as she handed me a birch bark wastebasket she had made. It reflected her careful artistic skill that I knew she had when she did my ironing. The basket is a work of art we treasure more than if it were made of gold foil.

* * * * *

Whenever I had dreamed of returning to Alaska, I was thinking of having close relationships with early settlers in the territory who had had experiences much like my family's. I envisioned friends sharing their experiences with me as I told of my family's early times. But we'd been gone twenty-three years, and things had certainly changed! The oil industry was luring hundreds of new residents with good-paying jobs. It was like a sockeye salmon expecting to return to a gentle stream only to find a raging torrent to navigate. The territory had become a state in 1959 and was now managing its own resources.

I knew the territory when the population was less than seventy-five thousand. Then we were not concerned with endangering the environment or exterminating a species. We made a very insignificant footprint, we thought. After all, there were almost eight square miles to each person in the territory. I thought one would have to be very reckless to ruin "his" eight square miles. Now, however, with a population of three hundred thousand, four times what it was when we left, there was a growing concern for saving the pristine wilderness and its resources. It was hard for me to realize that the vast resources could actually be depleted by this influx of people and technology. It was irritating, however, that the environmental movement was coming largely from Outside through folks who had never been to Alaska.

We'd learned of the excellent clam digging at Clam Gulch, just twenty miles south of Soldotna and were eager to harvest some. As I put the clam guns (shovels) in the VW Bug, I asked, "Gordon, do you know we need an Alaska State Fishing License to dig clams?" Not being allowed to just go out without a license anymore to dig clams at low tide was quite a surprise. It seemed it was going to be more difficult to live a subsistence lifestyle from the natural resources, which were now, in order to not deplete them, being regulated more than anyone living in the early territorial days could have imagined.

"The Last Frontier" was now being thought of as "The Last Wilderness." Newcomers didn't like it to be touched by man's ambitious business ventures.

Natural resources, I had thought, were riches just waiting to be mined, fished, or harvested in the most economical way. There had seemed to be such a vast amount of fish, trees, minerals, and game that they would never be depleted. That mind-set was what made me think of Alaska as the land of opportunity. As a young person, I joined many who welcomed huge companies to the territory to take advantage of the resources and thus provide jobs. We looked forward to the next boom when some large company came in with money to develop a new mine, start a pulp mill, or buy furs. Little thought was given to how our environment might be harmed. The booms were what made Alaska "the land of opportunity."

Sourdoughs (old-timers) who were happy with the status quo were hard to find among the cheechakos (newcomers) wanting change. In Soldotna the oil business was making a big impact; I went to visit my next door neighbor. The change in the population became very apparent to me when my neighbor replied to my question about what work her husband did by saying, "Oh, he works in the *all whales*." It took me a second to interpret her Oklahoma accent. She'd said "He works in the *oil wells*." I felt out of place. It dawned on me that I actually had traditions, relating to how to manage our natural resources, that I didn't want to let go of. I wasn't so different from my Midwest friends who loved traditions and wanted to do things in the same way forever.

* * * * *

At first, I thought all the concern for the environment was ridiculous. After reading Margaret Murie's book, *Two in the Far North*, about saving the Arctic from any commercial development, I got upset when reading about how much she loved the space, roughly the size of North Carolina, that she wanted to be left untouched by man: the Arctic National Wildlife Reserve (ANWR). *Who was she anyhow? How could she not see the economic value of, for instance, drilling for oil in this area? And now she'd moved from "our state" to live in Wyoming! If she loved Alaska and the ANWR area so much, why didn't she stay up here and enjoy it instead of trying to dictate to us, who live here, what should be done with it? Hardly anyone, anyway, was ever going to see the pristine ANWR, because it was too expensive to travel there.*

When we'd been in Soldotna two years, our daughter Carol and her husband, John, flew from Iowa for a visit. Gordon had earned a private pilot's license and was eager to take them up for a flight. The weather was a wonderful eighty degrees, a high almost unheard of in Southcentral Alaska. The day after their arrival, we flew across Cook Inlet to Tyonek to visit friends. When it was time to take off for our return, we could see that the tall trees at the end of the upwind runway made clearing them improbable. There was hardly a breath of wind, so we measured by walking the length of the runway to see whether we could take off with the wind. There appeared to be enough room and no trees to clear in that direction. We followed another plane taking off downwind. What we didn't know was that hot air has less lift to it. We stalled on takeoff and crashed onto the beach.

Rescuers were there almost immediately and ordered first responders from Anchorage. We were airlifted by helicopter to Anchorage Providence Hospital. I was unaware of all of this, because I'd suffered a severe concussion and was in a coma for four days. I have no recollection of that day or the one before when Carol and John arrived.

John was killed instantly on the impact. Gordon suffered broken ankles and facial lacerations. Carol had a broken back. The first prognosis for Carol was that she'd be a quadriplegic. In my foggy state I could hardly realize the consequences, but I thought, *Others have gone through similar tragedies and managed to live meaningful lives.* Each day, however, the doctor reported so much improvement that step-by-step, after six weeks, wearing only a small back brace, she walked out of the hospital. We attributed her miraculous healing to the amount of loving care and support we received. We got phone calls, letters, and visits and felt the love from folks from every place we'd ever lived. It seemed to me that it was like being lifted off my hospital bed.

The crash, of course, was attributed to "pilot error."

"How can you ever forgive me?" Gordon asked Carol.

"Dad, you're always forgiven," she answered. Her answer assured me that she'd learned a basic lesson of Christianity: grace. That gave me a comforting feeling of relief. Yet, knowing he was forgiven, the weight of this tragedy took a lot of energy from Gordon, and in 1978 he felt burned out. He resigned from Christ Lutheran Church.

Chapter 10

Return to First Love: Printing

We were not prepared financially to retire or to take that coveted and long-awaited trip to Germany, but when Gordon saw an ad offering Eagle River Printing for sale, he hesitatingly asked me what I thought about owning a print shop. I said he should go to Eagle River, a part of the Municipality of Anchorage, and look into it. When he came back, he was enthusiastically ready to go back to his first love: printing. With financial help from my folks we bought the shop in 1979.

Carol returned to Ankeny, Iowa, as soon as she was discharged from the hospital. She and John had just purchased a new home. Fortunately, they'd bought insurance that paid off the mortgage if either of them died.

Our younger daughter, Janet, had moved to Soldotna from Ketchikan before the accident and was working for Alaska Aeronautical Industries (AAI), a commuter plane service, so she was able to fly, on an employee's pass, to Anchorage whenever she needed to be with us during the six weeks it took us to be discharged from the hospital. It had been her job to notify all friends and relatives of our crash. Doing that seemed quite a burden for a twenty-one-year-old.

Janet's social life was enlivened by the attention of Frederick (Tex) Showalter, a skipper of one of the fisheries ships. They soon were married in November of 1977. His life away from home for nine months at a time, while crab fishing in the Bering Sea, was very lucrative but a strain on their marriage, and they divorced after six years. Tex is the father of her two sons Todd and Aaron.

Son Norman and his wife, Tracey, with their one-year-old son, Jason, moved to Soldotna after Norman's junior year at North Dakota State University. He worked on the North Slope as a bull cook who did housekeeping for the oil workers. His schedule was two weeks on and one week off. A year later Alicia was born in Anchorage. Wages for North Slope work were wonderfully high, and they saved money and planned to finance a new home, but the size of their family increased about as fast as ours had. Ethan was born two years after his sister. Savings were used up in welcoming new family members and buying investment property. The severe downturn in real estate in the early 1980s devastated their hopes for their future.

Since I was partially paralyzed on my left side from the concussion I got in the plane crash, I needed lots of physical therapy to gain back normal mobility. I wasn't able to substitute teach any longer, so I took accounting classes with tuition subsidized by Workman's Compensation.

When Eagle River Printing had been established a few years earlier by the owner of the building where it is located, the printing jobs were mostly brochures, stationery, business cards, and business forms, but shortly before we bought the shop they had put out an advertising map of Eagle River, which boosted their gross income substantially.

The printing process had changed dramatically since Gordon had worked full time at it in the '50s. Twenty-seven years before, printing was done from "hot type" or cast lead "slugs" assembled on a Linotype machine. Now everything was printed from metal sheets, with the material to be printed burned on them by photo engraving. Instead of Linotype machines, computers were what typesetters used. Gordon was not very familiar with the new process, but he knew what the outcome should be and learned quickly how to produce the jobs. He would say, "I never go to work. I just go to the shop to play with my toys."

Since the early days' income from the print shop wouldn't be enough to live on, I accepted a job with the Internal Revenue Service in Anchorage. Riding the bus to work in Anchorage was like joining an extended family. We visited and shared our life stories. If someone was absent some days, when they returned we all asked where they had been. This was quite the opposite of what I observed in San Francisco when I was sent there for two weeks of training. The same people waited for the Bay Area Rapid Transit (BART) each day, but they never spoke to one another, even when they were on board the rail. I was happy to return home to a more friendly atmosphere after the training.

After we'd had the print shop about five years, we decided to take a chance and start printing a monthly shopper with ads solely from Eagle River businesses. It would be mailed to every address in Eagle River and near-by Chugiak. We needed an advertising salesperson. I'd put in five years with the IRS, so I was ready for change. The shop was doing well enough that we didn't need my salary any more. I don't have a salesperson's convincing personality, but dutifully I went to every business to see if they wanted an ad. If I sold enough ads for a thirty-page issue of *The Cache*, we thought we were doing well because we could pay the postage and paper costs. Today with an excellent salesperson, *The Cache* often has seventy pages of advertising.

At first we were required to only give the post of-fice enough copies for each mailman to deliver one to everyone on his route. Soon the post office required that each paper have an address, but they wouldn't supply the addresses. We bought maps with the addresses indicated and typed the ten thousand addresses into the computer. Having done that, the post office fine-tuned the list, and we had a saleable mailing list for other bulk mailers.

When we bought the shop, it was equipped with two presses, a stitcher (stapler), a hand-powered cutter, and a folder as well as the darkroom camera and devel-oping paraphernalia. Gordon soon got tired of pulling the cutter's blade handle down and went shopping for an electric-powered machine. The volume of printing war-ranted one. Next project was to upgrade the folder to fold the many-paged Cache among other printing jobs. For years, a dream of Gordon's was to own a Heidelberg press, considered, in the trade, to be the "Cadillac," and after about fifteen years in business, he got his dream. He located a used two-color one in Portland that we could afford. Newer presses required much less make-ready time (getting the job ready to be printed) but this press still put out a good quality product.

We had a side business of making rubber address stamps. For this we had an old Linotype machine to make molds for the rubber. Sometimes I set a few lines on this too-out-of-date-for-printing machine. I'd been fascinated all my life by the intricacies of this genius of a machine whose arm came down to pick up the letter molds, dip them into the molten lead and then distribute the molds back into their special slots as a "slug" of "hot type," and then the rubber stamp mold came sliding out. The *chit, chit, chit* sound of the molds dropping into their slots brought back memories of my childhood when my folks published *The Alaska Sportsman* magazine. I was happy to be back in the industry again. One day I mused, *Oh, this is who I'm supposed to be!* I felt a freedom from the self-imposed role of playing what I thought a pastor's wife should be.

* * * * *

We had kept in touch with our exchange student son, Tig, in Ethiopia and felt bad that he was not able to go to school when the university was closed. We had considered him *our son*, and that relationship extended on, even when he returned to his original home. One year the birthday present check I'd sent him was returned marked "signature guaranteed." I couldn't figure out why Tig had not signed it as he had previous ones. Just at that time the movie *Holocaust* came out. It was about the Jews sent to concentration camps and disappearing,

189

and I was deeply moved and wondered why people didn't investigate their absence. I heard nothing from Tig. My letters were returned "undeliverable." I decided I couldn't just let him disappear like Jews in Germany had, so I contacted the Red Cross, the State Department, and every other organization that I thought would search for him. They produced no information.

But just then we got a letter from Tig in Sudan. He explained he'd joined the underground against the Ethiopian government and then found out the underground was just as corrupt as the government. So, being on the "wanted list" of both the underground and government, he fled to Sudan and was now ready to immigrate to the U.S.

I contacted our U.S. Representative, Don Young, and he expedited Tig's immigration to Eagle River. We paid for his travel, and he came with a refugee's green card, which allowed him to work for us at the print shop. We welcomed him like a prodigal son. It was so good to have him with us again. In a few months, however, he announced he had a scholarship to American University in Washington, D.C. and had made plans to attend in the fall.

His letters to us from the university were full of news of his progress, and he was soon ready to graduate with a degree in accounting. We went to his graduation and were guests of a couple who had taken a shine to Tig and helped him through school. Shortly after, he took the Certified Public Accountant exam and did not pass, which is a common outcome of first-time testing. I honestly think that was his first experience with major failure of any great importance.

He got a job as a taxi driver and didn't continue any education that we knew of. Whenever I called him, he had a new phone number and address. In fact he was moving very frequently, and it seemed he didn't want me to contact him nor did he follow up on a Minnesota hospital job opportunity I told him about. Again, I thought, *What a waste of a mind!*

We lost contact with him. This time I hired a private detective to find him. The detective located him and interviewed him, not letting on that I had hired him. I learned he'd borrowed several thousand dollars from my aunt Florence that he'd never paid back.

I didn't try to talk to him nor write to him anymore. Recently, I googled his name and found out he'd died in Maryland at age fifty-five. My efforts to find out the cause of his death have not been fruitful. *Did he get involved with drugs?* That is the only plausible explanation I can think of. I have been unsuccessful in contacting the county coroner.

* * * * *

During the twenty years we owned the print shop, we experienced tough times and good ones too. During one period we got behind on our payments, and the former owner, Tony DeLucia, came in to see what the matter was. After we took the corrective steps he suggested to streamline the business, he made an offer we couldn't refuse. He and his wife, Sandra, would come in and work free until we got caught up! They helped us save the business. *What a difference from the absence of any solutions to our problems in Moose Lake!*

We joined the Lutheran Church of Hope in Anchorage. In 1982 they were in the process of sponsoring an

Amerasian Korean who, because he was not "pure Korean," had little chance of a successful future in his country. Persons like him, whose father was American, were considered "disabled" and not fit for military service, for instance. All the necessary paperwork had been done, but the signature of an individual sponsor was needed. We volunteered to sign and thus be his first Alaska "parents."

Peter Park was thirty years old. He lived with us for several weeks and was eager to fit in. Later he lived with several other members of the church, but he always called us Mom and Dad. His green card permitted him to work as soon as he arrived, and work he did! In just a few years he had saved enough money to return to Korea and bring back a lovely wife, Angela. Within ten years he became part owner of a printing company in Anchorage, and he, Angela, and their two boys became citizens. At their naturalization ceremony Peter made "Bordine" his middle name, to honor us.

The family has thrived and owns their own home. Angela is an interpreter for the Anchorage School District. Brandon, the oldest son won a huge scholarship to the University of Pennsylvania where he earned an electrical engineering degree. Matthew is attending the University of Alaska Anchorage. When the print shop he had invested in sold, Peter became a truck driver for Lynden Transport. Our busy lives don't make it easy to get together often, but Peter contacts us and brings gifts on special days.

Like me, Janet had married a printer, Doug Boyer. When Doug had worked for us a short time, Gordon decided to retire, and Janet and Doug bought the business.

Chapter 11

Shishmaref Calling

Gordon went to the bishop of the Alaska Synod of Evangelical Lutheran Church in America (ELCA) and asked if he could help the church in any way. The reply was "How would you like to be interim pastor at Shishmaref, Alaska?" What an opportunity! We both were excited at the possibility. The Inupiat village of about six hundred people was familiar to us because we had read Sunday school stories about the church's establishment there, north of Nome on the Seward Peninsula, about seven hundred miles northwest of Anchorage and only accessible by plane.

As we were about to land at "Shish" in the commuter plane, I could see the village was built on a barrier island of sand about a fourth of a mile wide and, maybe, three miles long. I spotted the church on the north end of the island on the highest spot. Were it not for the various erosion-prevention objects along the beach, the white sand could have been mistaken for a California beach.

Our plane set down at the airport where I saw the lagoon to the east and the Chukchi Sea on the west. A truck, the only vehicle besides four-wheelers (ATV, all terrain vehicles) in the village, soon came to take us to the parsonage beside the church. I was most pleasantly surprised by the spacious living quarters with huge picture windows that looked out on the beautiful lagoon with mountains behind it. Several large skiffs floated near shore. What I didn't see were trees. Only bushes could survive this far north. They and grass kept sand from eroding in the wind, but it was the sea that was taking its toll on the west side of the island. Erosion was evident along the sandy beach that stretched the whole length of the island where the ocean had gnawed away at the bluffs. Since the island itself was one big sand pile, the ocean was a continued menacing predator.

The parsonage was modern in every way except for running water. That was only obtainable from the village washeteria, where we could shower on assigned days for men and women, wash clothes, and fill our water buckets. Once Gordon forgot it was men's shower day, and his next chance for a shower was in a week.

A highly-respected elder had died just before our arrival, so his funeral was one of Gordon's first responsibilities. Since there was no funeral home closer than the forty-five-minute flight to Nome, it was the family's duty to prepare the body. This was done in the arctic entry (the body shop) to the church basement. The body lay on cardboard from flattened boxes when Gordon was summoned to tie the man's tie. It is quite a challenge to tie someone else's tie, let alone one belonging to a man whose funeral was scheduled for the next day.

The church was packed for the funeral. I thought Gordon's words of encouragement were some of the most endearing I'd heard. The choir sang in their language of

Inupiaq. Everyone at the funeral service processed to the graveyard beside the parsonage. As the casket was being lowered, they realized the excavation was too short for it to fit, so some men quickly jumped down into it and shoveled more sand until the box fit.

The church owned a four-wheeler with a small trailer big enough to haul our laundry and water. I quickly learned to drive it and thought it was great fun. If I got stuck in the sand, I soon heard "Do you need any help?" Someone was always quick to stop what they were doing and help.

Fetching water and taking showers in the washeteria soon became routine. We used a "honey bucket" at home in lieu of a regular toilet. This refuse was picked up regularly after we placed it outside. We were responsible for taking our other refuse to the dump at the south end of the island.

On our first run to the dump we ran out of gas. Luckily a twelve-year-old boy was near. He came over on his bicycle and showed us how to switch to the reserve tank of gas. As we drove on, we noticed him, hovering nearby on his own small ATV, making sure we didn't get into any other trouble. He'd already learned to take care of elders. We felt loved.

The laundering routine: I took the clothes to the washeteria to use the clothes washers. When they were clean, I brought the clothes home in a black garbage bag to be dried in the clothes dryer in the parsonage kitchen. On one garbage run, my clean wet clothes sat next to the black bags filled with garbage in the kitchen. Mistaking the laundry bag for garbage, Gordon loaded it into the little trailer, and we proceeded to the dump where we threw it out. The next day I discovered the error, and we hurriedly returned to the dump. Sure enough, there was the still-closed bag of clean clothes frozen solid from the freezing night. When we told Janet of this episode, she soon mailed us a hand-sewn cloth laundry bag with "Washing! Not garbage!" on it in large letters.

By the time we left in November, I had learned all the steps required to produce clean clothes. I thought I had the washeteria laundry routine down pat after several weeks, but on one trip I fouled up in several ways. I got to the facility without any problem but discovered I'd forgotten to bring money or tokens for the washing machine. I hurried back the couple of blocks to pick up some money. On the return to the washeteria, my trailer came loose, and I had to have help hitching it up. Then when I got to my destination, I found I'd not brought soap. Back to the parsonage I went. This time I made the three-block trip without trouble.

I was thrilled to actually live where people dried their meat on fish racks like I'd seen in pictures all my life. One day while talking to an elder near a fish rack, I noticed not only fish drying but also a reindeer skin, seal skins, and some thin brown sheets. Thinking these thin sheets might be a seal's stomach or some other such exotic material, I asked my friend what it was. "Oh, we call that 'plastic,'" he said. They were actually sheets of common plastic just hanging out to dry. Was my face red? I'm sure the whole village got a big laugh out of that and so did I. I think I enjoyed making dumb mistakes as much as the villagers who witnessed them.

One morning I saw many neighbors heading down the "iron road" (the main road that was reinforced with metal plates like those used on remote landing strips) toward the south end of the island. *What was going on?* We had to find out.

As we were starting up our four-wheeler, a neighbor stopped his ATV with three of his kids hanging on. "Come on down to the inlet. We got a whale!" he yelled above the motor noise.

Shishmaref is off the whales' migration route, and they don't often hunt whale, so we wondered how they happened to harvest one now. We learned this gray whale, swimming off the usual route, was close to the village when it was spotted. It took some scrambling to get together what was necessary to harvest the animal. After it was hit dozens of times with a smaller gun than usually used in whaling, the whale gave itself to the hunters.

Half the village was gathered around the huge carcass when we got there. Men were standing on top of it, slicing blubber with their sharp long-handled cutting tools. The big suitcase-sized blocks of blubber were being laid out on a blue tarp for later distribution: first to elders. Several women were slicing up finger-sized samples of *maktak* (whale skin and blubber, what we often hear as "muktuk"). "Here, help yourselves!" they invited. With mixed feelings, we helped ourselves and felt honored to be included in the sharing, yet hesitant to taste this unique food. Gordon was chewing like a moose gorging on willow branches as fat juice rolled down his chin. I was satisfied with nibbling on one piece, but Gordon liked the treat and ate several more.

That afternoon, several pounds of whale meat were delivered to us. This was different from the blubber and was much like beef meat in flavor and texture. We enjoyed many meals of whale steaks smothered in onions.

Knowing that the village didn't have a quota assigned by the International Whaling Commission for the number of whales they were allowed to catch, I asked an elder whose quota it would be included in. "Wales? Barrow? Wainwright? Point Hope?"

"Naw," he replied, chuckling. "Nobody's. We're all going to jail tomorrow!"

A man after my own heart, I thought. *That's one way to deal with unwanted regulations!*

Later in the summer we were very popular at our family reunion in Michigan because we had brought an ample supply of the little blubber samples to share, like we'd had on the Shishmaref beach.

We enjoyed a variety of wild game because of what the villagers shared with us. Gifts of salmon were plentiful, and we had moose and reindeer meat as well as the whale meat for many meals.

We had arrived in Shishmaref in early July 1997, and were comfortable wearing short-sleeved tee shirts on our ATV rides to the post office to pick up boxes we'd mailed to ourselves from Anchorage. This was no indication of what was to come in October.

On one of those blistery fall days, our daily walk reminded me of our stormy-weather dates in Ketchikan when we walked long past my curfew. Then, the rain in our faces and dripping down our slickers meant we could enjoy each other in such weather we were together. I'd felt euphoric.

As we walked the iron road in the village, the desperate look on the face of a woman struggling to stand against the wind told us her feelings about the storm were opposite of ours on those on our romantic hikes during storms years before. Now the storm threatened to undercut homes and send them toppling to the beach below. We soon came upon one small house with half of it hanging over the cliff.

Waves were beating away at the cliff like they were hungry wolves gnawing on a rabbit's hind quarters. Several other buildings would soon be digested by the surf. We were told this was the most ravenous storm in many years.

The phone rang the next day. "Are you alright?" Bishop Parsons wanted to know. "The TV here in Anchorage has been full of news of how bad the storm is."

"We're fine. Since we're on the highest part of the island, the storm isn't a threat here, but it's endangering so many homes that the National Guard is coming to help the emergency services people."

Before the storm abated, a C-130 National Guard plane brought heavy equipment to move the armory and other buildings. TV Channel 2 from Anchorage, about one thousand miles southeast, had reporters on the scene. A total of eleven homes were moved to safer ground, and there were plans to move others in the near future. Governor Knowles declared the village a disaster area and appropriated three million dollars for relief. We joined villagers who were hired to fill sand bags used to discourage the monster waves from chewing the cliff away. Our Honda ATV was assigned to emergency services for several days.

Erosion had been a problem for decades but is now an urgent one since we've left. Solutions include building a huge bulwark or moving the village. Erosion control has been attempted by dumping huge boulders, cement blocks, and any large item such as vehicles, refrigerators, and oil tanks along the beach. The ocean licked the sand around the edges of the fill, and soon it was inefficient. Moving the village from its ancient and convenient hunting spot would not only be a very expensive project monetarily but also one costly in human heritage and welfare when hunters would have to expend more energy in providing food. The villagers are expected to take their time discussing which plan is the best and then decide on a new location for the village if they choose to move.

Shortly after the storms, we learned our interim assignment would soon be over because Pastor Timothy and Synje Oslovich had accepted the call to Shishmaref and would come from the East Coast about November first. It was good to know that the congregation would shortly have a permanent pastor who could make his own plans for ministry. We had not begun any long-range programs, since we believed the permanent pastor shouldn't be locked into programs he might not be comfortable with.

* * * * *

When we talked to Bishop Parsons about our experiences, we told him we'd felt warmly welcomed and had enjoyed working and learning with the people. "Isn't it wonderful how accepting they are?" he replied. "How would you like to fill in at Nome for a few months? They are just beginning the call process now. I don't know how long you'd be needed there."

Was it a miracle that we'd have another chance to be in Nome after turning back that call when we'd just arrived in Moose Lake? It didn't take long to make an affirmative decision. With the Oslovichs on their way, we were settled in Nome by the end of October. The parsonage, a ranch house with four bedrooms, was beside the A-frame church building. Everything in Nome was within walking distance, but it seemed like a pretty large city to us after making the small jaunts around Shishmaref.

The Nome congregation was made up of Native Inupiat and non-Native folks. Most of the Natives had come from other Seward Peninsula villages and many were related to Shishmaref people. We marveled at the huge church building. Its beautiful A-frame design suggested it could have been dropped in directly from the Midwest, where such church-building plans were the norm. Here the high ceiling made heating bills soar.

Beautiful Christian symbols sewn from hair seal hung behind the altar, distinguishing it as a Native church.

Back in Eagle River at the print shop, Doug was in a bind. He didn't have a pressman to run *The Cache*. Since we got to Nome a few days early, Gordon was able to fly down, a three-hour flight, and run the issue for him and return the next day.

We got bad news soon after he returned. Gordon's brother, Keith, called to tell us that their mother in Michigan was not doing well, and it would be a good idea if Gordon flew back to see her. After Sunday services, Gordon flew off to Detroit where Keith met him, and they drove to Coldwater to be with their mother. She rallied upon seeing Gordon, but within a few days she suffered a stroke and passed on November 11. Gordon stayed until after the funeral.

Nome is made up of especially interesting people. It is a hub for the surrounding area and is visited by people of varied backgrounds with unique tasks who sometimes come to the church for information or help, such as a ride to the airport. One such person was Californian Dr. John Hultin, returning from Brevig Mission where he'd had permission to exhume the corpse of a person who had died in the influenza epidemic of 1918. He'd harvested some tissue from which he hoped to obtain the DNA of the virus that killed her. He would use it in his California lab for research on the H5N1 flu virus.

The congregation met several times during the call process, deciding what strong points a new pastor should have, and then considered the names of several who might be available. Evidently forgetting the successful missionary work of Helen Frost some seventy years before, they decided against calling a woman. Their decision was Pastor Frank Macht, who accepted the call and would come before June 1, 1998.

Soon after the first of the year, folks in Nome began making plans for the finish of the 1,059-mile Iditarod Dog Sled Dog Race from Anchorage to Nome that would end in March. Hundreds of people would be coming to town for the event. We decided to rent a room in the church addition to Iditarod fans. The profit from the B & B venture would go to the church. I had made plans, however, to go to the Arctic Winter Games in

Yellowknife, Northwest Territories, Canada, to cheer on my grandson, Aaron, in the speed skating races. We solved the problem of who would host the B & B folks by flying in Aaron's brother, Todd, an experienced food service employee from Eagle River. The net profit from that venture was over one thousand dollars.

Still dreaming of a European trip, I spent all my spare time in Nome researching travel plans. Following my requests for them, tour brochures by the dozens arrived. Gordon didn't show a lot of interest in my research. When Carol found out he wasn't much interested in extensive travel in Europe, she admonished him. "Dad, Mom has moved and followed you all these forty-seven years; now it's your turn to go where she wants to be."

I envisioned this trip to be our *one and only* across "the pond," so we should make the most of it. I had been intrigued by Gordon's cousin's family camping in a VW camper all through Europe and thought this would be the most economical and practical way to go. I located a van to lease in Switzerland. If we left in the fall, we could cover the warmer countries through spring and then head north to Sweden, the country of my heritage.

We could barely afford the trip, but as interim pastor we received not only that salary but were also getting social security benefits and had been able, at last, to save for travel.

Gordon's last Sunday in Nome was May 31, 1998. We were glad to be back home in Eagle River but left in July for a Bordine/Hoopingarner family reunion in Michigan. At Gideon Lake, outside Coldwater, the cousins, all in their sixties or older, replayed their youthful games of trying to stay underwater the longest and surprising the women with underwater shenanigans.

Chapter 12

Change in Travel Plans

Home again, I made final plans for being in Europe almost a year. We located a house sitter who was visiting family and in need of housing such as ours. We reserved the camping van to lease and bought tickets to Zurich for September 10.

We planned to celebrate our forty-seventh wedding anniversary on August 31 by going to Land's End Resort in Homer for a couple days. Gordon had seemed agreeable to all these plans and helped in the preparations. What was *not* in our plans was the event of August 30.

Hearing his feeble voice from our bedroom, I hurried down the hall, but Gordon came stumbling into the living room before I got very far. "I think I'm having a heart attack," he gasped. I called his doctor and told him Gordon's symptoms: shortness of breath, excessive sweating, et cetera and was told to call 911. The ambulance came in just a few minutes. Gordon was still conscious and could answer the medic's questions as they hurried off to Providence Hospital in Anchorage.

I followed within a short time. By the time I arrived, they had "scoured out" his artery, putting in a stint to hold his artery open, but he was still in too much pain, so they got his permission to do a heart bypass. Encouraged by having heard of the success of such an operation done on one of his Nome parishioners, Gordon was quick to say he wanted them to do that procedure.

Janet and Doug had notified Gordon's brother, Keith, and then Norman and Carol's families of the seriousness of Gordon's situation. In the recovery room after the operation, Gordon mumbled his name when asked, but that was his last response. Keith and his wife, Betty, arrived as did Norman and Carol. Hoping for some communication, we squeezed Gordon's hands and toes, told him of every little event, and asked him questions. There was no reaction. He remained comatose, but from his facial expression appeared completely comfortable and at peace. This went on for four weeks.

Finally, the speech therapist suggested I tell him not to try so hard to wiggle his toes or squeeze our hands; he should just relax, and that I would be okay. In the privacy of his curtained area, I told him what had been suggested. I don't know if he heard me, but I heard myself say I'd be okay, and that was very comforting to me.

After four weeks we met with the doctors and our pastors, and we all agreed that with the prognosis being "he'd probably never be better than he was at this time," and with his life-long desire to be of service, life support should be ended. He passed away two days later with Pastor Tim Oslovich, who happened to be in town from Shishmaref, singing hymns to him. I thought, *Now he's going to experience what he's been preaching about these past twenty years.*

The memorial service at Joy Lutheran Church Eagle River was most comforting with a dozen of our pastor friends, donned in their clergy vestments, participating. Over a hundred friends and relatives listened as a remembrance was shared about happy times spent in our Moose Lake sauna when couples would come to our house. Problems of the world had been solved by the men in that sauna and by the women who visited in our kitchen while waiting for their husbands. A display of pictures along with his ink-soiled printing overalls and clergy robe with stole were witness to Gordon's life of service. In lieu of vocal sharing, mourners recalled their fondest memories of Gordon on note paper we provided. We have treasured these thoughts ever since. A special one by a second-grader testified, "He taught me to whistle."

Janet and I drove the seven hundred fifty miles north to Wiseman to spread Gordon's ashes. Wiseman was a favorite place of his, because he loved to picture and muse about my Grandpa August's life there, searching in vain for gold. We spread his ashes in the cemetery among many old-timers' graves. We thought it was a place among pioneers that he would appreciate.

* * * * *

I set out to be *all right*. I was still thinking of a European trip. I wouldn't rent a camping van but travel by commercial means. In the spring of 1999, I set out on a ninety-day trip, thinking this would be my *one and only* trip across the Atlantic. I started out with a tour of Turkey and stopped in thirteen different countries going as far north as the Norwegian ferry goes to Kirkenes, before heading south through Sweden to cousin Carl-Erik Mawe's family.

I'm sometimes asked if I was scared to travel alone. On the contrary, I found fellow travelers and local citizens to be very helpful. It was easy, too, to strike up conversation when traveling alone. I seldom had trouble communicating, because almost everyone I spoke to could speak English. Knowing only English, however, made me often feel inadequate.

One outstanding incident of generosity was when I was traveling from Poland to Czech Republic on a second-class train ticket. I had trouble finding the second-class railroad car. My suitcase got heavier and heavier. Sweat flowed down my face like the Yukon River breakup. Finally I gave up and entered the compartment of a first-class car. An older couple was already comfortably settled in. It was probably their private space, but I didn't know any better. I figured when the conductor came along she could direct me to my proper area.

The couple welcomed me in, stowed my heavy bag on the rack above, and we began to get acquainted. They were from Germany, traveling to Israel for health care. When I told them I was from Alaska, they asked if I'd ever seen a bear, so I began relating the many bear-viewing adventures I'd had. They tried to envision seeing as many as a hundred black bear that I'd seen in one day at the Naha Falls, Loring, Alaska, near Ketchikan. Soon they shared a sandwich with me. After I'd told several bear stories, the conductor came to collect tickets. I asked where the second-class car was because I didn't have the cash to pay the extra to remain in the first-class compartment. "Oh, don't go now!" the German gentleman said, as he reached for his wallet and pulled out enough German marks to pay the difference for a first-class ticket. Most pleasantly shocked, I accepted his offer and settled back down to recall more bear adventure stories for their pleasure.

"Where are you staying in Prague?" my benefactor asked.

Pointing to a hotel with a low room rate indicated in my *Lonely Planet* guide book, I said "I think I'll stay here."

"That should be OK. Do you have a reservation?"

"No, I don't think I'll need one this time of year."

As he pulled his cell phone from his shirt pocket he said, "I'll make a reservation for you."

Using the number listed in the *Lonely Planet*, he dialed but seemed frustrated. It was a number no longer in service. He persisted, following the voice mail instructions and finally succeeded in making a reservation for me.

With their promises of visiting me in Alaska someday, we parted in Prague. I am still hoping to be able to take them on their own bear-sighting adventure.

Another time, when my lack of experience in travel got me in trouble, I was immediately helped by another passenger. I was boarding a train in Germany when I plopped down in an empty seat. Soon a nice gentleman informed me that I was in his reserved seat. I'd not known I should reserve myself a seat. When he realized how naive I was, he hurried off to another empty place, saying he liked that one better because it had Internet access.

When we reached my destination, he asked if I had a place to stay. When I said I didn't, he got off the train with me, located a red cap and told him in German to take me to the concierge who would help me find suitable housing. Then, as he got back on the train to continue his trip, he gave me some coins to tip the red cap for his service.

In Sweden, Carl-Erik Mawe's daughter-in-law, Margareta, picked me up and drove me to their summer house several hours away. On the way there, she stopped so I could tour a restored ancient Swedish village, which included an ancient church. How good it felt to enjoy the Carl-Erik-style hugs from his son, Ulf, Karin's dad. At their summer house, Margareta and her daughter Karin, who had visited me in Eagle River, saw to it that I "passed" the sauna exam: I'd not exited before the others. I'd never felt so clean nor "honest" as in this condition. I'd never been tempted to use our Moose Lake sauna, because I remembered how I suffered during the 110-degree days in Decorah, Iowa.

In Denmark, I phoned Karl Rye and his wife, Barbara. Karl was the oldest of the Rye children with whom we'd been close friends at Luther College. He had been working in Copenhagen, and they were on their way to her mother's home in Silt, off the northern coast of Germany. They told me where I could meet them and continue on with them to Silt. What a wonderful several days I spent at Barbara's mother's home on this picturesque resort island! Many of the homes had thatched roofs like those in Ireland. I felt like I was with family because they welcomed me as if I were a relative. It was good, too, to visit with someone (Karl) who had English as their first language.

We had renewed contact, after fifteen years, with the Rye family a short time before my trip. Carol had read in a school paper that Kjell Rye had designed the gym floor mosaic for one of the Lake Washington District's schools where she worked. *This can only be Kjell Rye, the youngest son of our Luther College friends, the Ryes*, she thought. When she called Kjell, he told her his brother Karl and wife lived in Palmer, Alaska, only twenty miles from Eagle River. Gordon and I had quickly contacted them and renewed our friendship. Karl had since obtained work in Denmark for Siemens. Karl's mother, Miry, soon relocated in Alaska near us too.

I surprised everyone and even myself a year after I returned home. I took the opportunity to join Rotarians on a trip to India for National Immunization Day to assist in Rotary's program to stamp out polio from the world. Evidently my ninety-day trip was not to be my *one and only* to foreign lands. In India, I thought, *Here I am, almost fifty years after Aunt Florence's visit, essentially working toward putting the prosthesis manufacturing company, she had started, out of business because its products would not be in great demand when polio is wiped out of the country.*

My next long trip was with a friend on a tour of China, taking in not only the Great Wall and the Terra-Cotta Army but virtually every place I'd ever heard of in the country. We certainly got our money's worth during the twenty-one-day trip. I was interested in the efforts of the government to train their citizens to queue and not break in front of persons waiting for service. They were particularly interested in making a good impression for the Olympic Games.

211

One summer, Carol and I visited our Luther College friends, Walt and Marian Cherwien, who had rented a vacation villa in southern France. Walt had retired from his position as a French language teacher in Minnesota. It was nice to have Walt, who was proficient in French, tour us around southeast France. The countryside was certainly different from China's. France was pastoral while the Chinese seemed to be hustling everywhere.

Most recently, Janet, Carol, and I visited Sweden where relatives again were the most gracious hosts. The girls and I visited the estate where Grandma Emma grew up. The baron's home is still there and is now a five-star restaurant. We had hoped to have lunch there, but it happened to be closed that day. The owner, however, gave us a tour of this elite venue.

We went on to visit Käringön. The little island where Grandpa August grew up is now a vacation destination. The church where he worshipped was still in use and is in pristine condition. One could easily imagine Pastor Simson preaching from the lofty pulpit as if he himself were God. Pastor Simson's grave was in the cemetery beside the church.

My cousin, Bjorn Tobin, was our generous host. A major surprise was to meet three-year-old Theo Tobin, Bjorn's grandson. He is a mirror image of Janet's oldest son, Todd, when he was that age. We had thought Todd inherited his looks from his father's side of the family. We are looking forward to these relatives visiting us in Alaska.

I haven't made three trips around the world like Aunt Florence did, but I certainly am grateful for the traveling I've done. I only wish Gordon could have been with me.

We always had such good times traveling. I longed for European travel all of my adult life until, at age, sixty-nine, I made that first trip overseas. Since then, I've enjoyed seven international journeys. When someone asks if I've been to a particular country I haven't visited, I usually reply, "No, I haven't been there yet."

Epilogue

Janet and Doug have sold Eagle River Printing and will retire to Idaho in 2013. That means all three of our children will be in the Pacific Northwest, so I will soon move to Vancouver, Washington, to be near them. Leaving Alaska will not be easy, but I am familiar with Vancouver since it is where my parents retired. Leaving close friends here in Eagle River will be as tough as it was for my folks to leave Ketchikan friends when they retired.

The Alaska Gordon and I left in 1952 has changed to become less frontier and a more modern-living atmosphere. Visitors expect the pampered treatment the big cruise lines offer while still trying to experience The Last Frontier. Mom and Pop business ventures have given way to chain stores that provide everything necessary to live like the folks Outside do. Subsistence living gets to be a more and more difficult way of life. At my age, I enjoy these changes that make life easier.

But as I leave Alaska, my home and my ancestors' home for a total of one hundred fourteen years, I take with me all my memories and family history that comfort me. I am also comforted knowing that there is still one member of my family that is making his home in Alaska. Janet's younger son, Aaron Showalter, continues to work for the State of Alaska and travels to many places in the state with his job. He is having the experience of working in areas as remote as his Great-Great-Grandfather August did in Wiseman those many years ago.

Cabin built by Doris and Gordon Bordine past the end of North Tongass Highway, Ketchikan.

The Bordines' 1964 camping trip takes them to Washington, D.C. to visit their Minnesota representative. From the top: Gordon, Doris, Gloria Brown, Janet, Carol, Billy Mitchell, Norman, and Minnesota Representative Odin Langen.

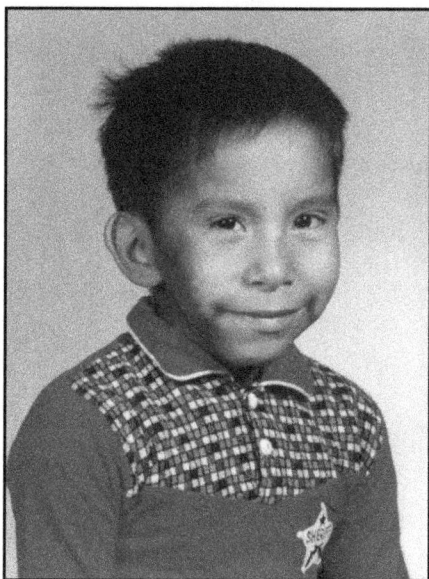

Billy Mitchell, 6, came into the Bordine family as their foster child in 1961 from the Leech Lake Indian Reservation.

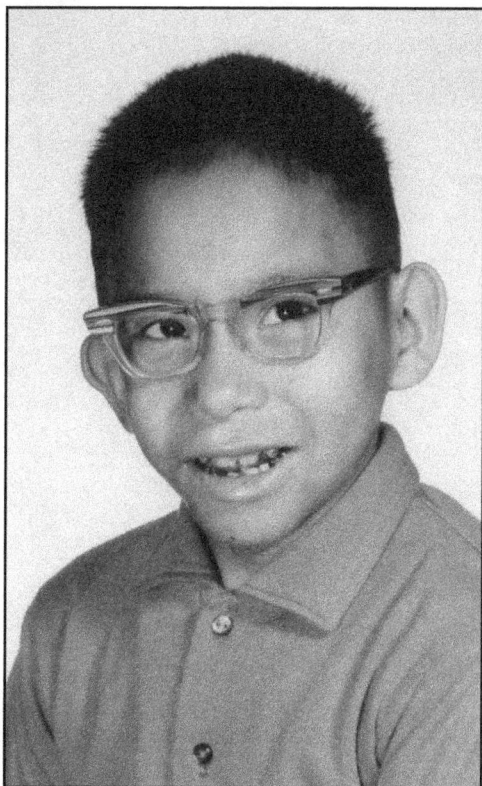

Billy Mitchell, our foster child, lived with the Bordines for ten years in Remer and Moose Lake, Minnesota.

View from the Bordine Island Lake home, Moose Lake, Minnesota, 1964

Billy Mitchell, our foster child, helps Norman get ready for the prom, 1970.

The Bordine family 1969. Front: Doris, Gordon. Back: Carol, Norman, Janet, and Billy Mitchell

The Bordine family 1971: Back: Billy Mitchell, Janet, Norman. Front: Teigistu Lemma, American Field Service Ethiopian Exchange Student, Doris, Gordon, and Carol.

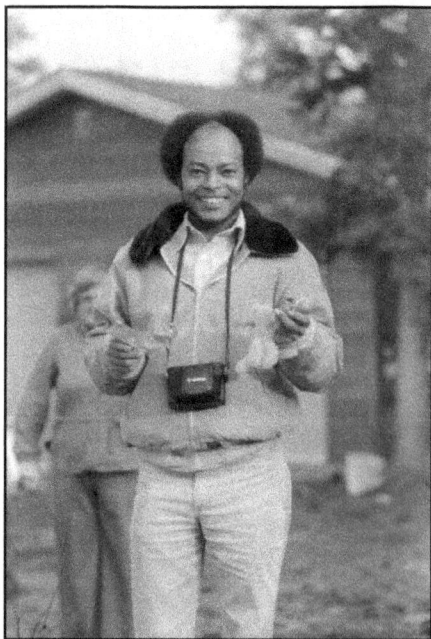

Teigistu Lemma, Ethiopian exchange student, celebrates Easter in Soldotna, Alaska, 1976.

Doris dresses like a native Turk in Turkey, 1999.

Doris points toward Alaska from a local artist's seaside monument in Käringön, Sweden, 1999.

ORDER FORM

I would like to order my own or another copy of the book *The Flip of a Coin* by Doris Tobin Bordine. Please send me:

\# books x \$15.95 per copy =   _____

\+ Postage (first class) & handling @ \$4.95/book: _____

TOTAL ENCLOSED   \$ _____

We accept cash, check, or money order made out to Northbooks, or VISA, Mastercard. Prices subject to change without notice.

(You may phone your VISA/MC order to Northbooks at 907-696-8973)

VISA/MC card \# ☐☐☐☐ ☐☐☐☐ ☐☐☐☐ ☐☐☐☐

Exp. date: ___ / ___   Amount charged: \$ _____

Signature: _____

Phone number: _____

Please send my book (s) to:

Name: _____

Address: _____

City: _____ State: _____ Zip: _____

Fill out this order form and send to:

Northbooks

11915 Lazy Street, Ste. C
Eagle River, AK 99577-7898
(907) 696-8973
www.northbooks.com

www.ingramcontent.com/pod-product-compliance
Lightning Source LLC
Chambersburg PA
CBHW031833090426
42741CB00005B/232